# Basic Materials in Music Theory

# Basic Materials in Music Theory:
# A Programed Course

## The Fourth Edition

**Paul O. Harder**

*Dean for Academic Administration*
*California State College, Stanislaus*

Allyn and Bacon, Inc.
Boston    London    Sydney    Toronto

**Library of Congress Cataloging in Publication Data**

Harder, Paul O
   Basic materials in music theory.

   Includes index.
   1. Music—Theory—Programmed instruction. I. Title
MT6.H255B4  1978      781'.07'7      77-22459
ISBN 0-205-06045-5

# Contents

*Preface to the Fourth Edition*     *vii*

*To the Student*     *ix*

*1*     *The Basic Materials of Music: Time and Sound*                                                    1

Time and sound · Sound waves · Pitch · Intensity · Amplitude ·
Timbre · The natural harmonic series · Partials and overtones · Duration

*2*     *The Notation of Pitch*                                                                                                     10

The staff · Notes: symbols for tones · The basic scale · The treble
clef · The bass clef · The C-clefs · Ledger lines · The grand staff ·
The *ottava* sign · Half- and whole-steps · Accidentals · Enharmonic
notes · The chromatic scale · Pitch designations

*3*     *Time Classification*                                                                                                        42

The beat · Meter · Simple and compound time · Borrowed divisions ·
Subdivision of the beat

*4*     *Note and Rest Values*                                                                                                    62

The relative value of notes and rests · The dot · Division of dotted and
undotted notes and rests · Subdivision of dotted and undotted notes and
rests · The unit in simple and compound time · Metronome indications ·
Terms which express tempo

*5*     *Time Signatures*                                                                                                           87

Time signatures in simple and compound time · The relation of time
signatures to time classification · Common time · *Alla breve* · The
tie · Rhythmic patterns · Syncopation

*6    Intervals*                                                          112

> Harmonic and melodic intervals · The numerical classification of intervals ·
> Compound intervals · The classification of intervals by quality · The
> inversion of intervals · Enharmonic intervals

*7    The Basic Scales*                                                    142

> Structure of the basic scales · Modes · The keynote

*8    The Major Scale*                                                     152

> Structure of the major scale · The use of accidentals to form major scales
> on any note

*9    The Minor Scales*                                                    162

> The natural minor scale · The harmonic minor scale · The melodic minor
> scale · Diatonic and chromatic intervals

*10    Key Signatures*                                                     187

> Key and tonality · Major key signatures · Relative keys · Minor key
> signatures · The use of accidentals to form the various minor scales ·
> The circle of fifths · Enharmonic keys · Parallel keys

*11    Triads*                                                             220

> The tertian system · Basic triads    Major triads · Minor triads ·
> Diminished triads · Augmented triads

*Appendix A:*    Glossary of Musical Terms                                 245

*Appendix B:*    Supplementary Assignments                                 251

*Appendix C:*    Eartraining Tips                                          283

*Index*                                                                    303

# Preface to the Fourth Edition

Musical styles of the twentieth century have led us far beyond the technical resources of "traditional" music. Why, then, should we learn facts which relate to music that is not only decades, but centuries old? The answer is that the study of traditional materials is as relevant now as in the past. Music based on the major-minor scale system, harmonic tonality, and metrical rhythms constitutes a large share of the music played and heard today. Many contemporary composers draw on a wide range of materials and techniques, tonal as well as atonal, ancient as well as modern, Western as well as non-Western. A knowledgeable approach to today's music is impossible without a thorough grounding in music fundamentals, which continue to provide the basis for musical understanding. Serious study of music, even the ability to converse knowingly about music, requires a command of musical terminology. The ability to read, write, and aurally apprehend musical structures such as intervals, scales, and triads is a prerequisite for musical training.

What are the fundamentals of music? In order to communicate with others about music, it is necessary to possess a common vocabulary. Music fundamentals provide the basis for this vocabulary. It is true that musical terminology is not completely standardized, but in this book the most widely accepted terms are used. The eleven chapters contain the basic grammar of music, but stop short of functional matters such as the relationship of chords to a key center and to one another. This is reserved for the study of tonal harmony. The emphasis here is on the ordering of time and sound, the two basic properties of music:

1. The musical structures related to time are beat, meter, note values, rhythmic patterns, and time signatures.

2. The musical structures related to sound are the staff, clef signs, notes, intervals, scales, triads, and key signatures.

This book employs a learning system called *programed instruction*. This method results in quick, thorough learning, with little or no help required from the instructor. Students can work as rapidly or as slowly as they desire, and can repeat any set of drills as many times as is necessary to achieve mastery. Students themselves can immediately check the correct solution to questions and drills. In this way, comprehension of the material is subject to constant evaluation; a missed concept or an error of judgment is isolated quickly, before damage is done.

Because this book provides self-paced learning, and requires little supplementation, it is ideal for a quick review before proceeding with more advanced work, for use in the applied studio, for individual study, and as the beginning text in a course devoted to the study of tonal harmony.

The fourth edition contains a series of aural exercises called *Eartraining Tips*. These exercises make suggestions regarding eartraining experiences which students can provide for themselves. The goal is to broaden comprehension of the factual material presented in the text. A musical fact is only half learned through intellectual comprehension; aural recognition is equally necessary.

The organization and methods of this book reflect the experimentation and free exchange of ideas carried out over a period of many years by the theory faculty at Michigan State University. I am especially indebted to the many students and teachers who have made suggestions based on actual learning and teaching experiences. Their suggestions have assisted greatly in refining the methods now employed in this book.

*Paul Harder*

# To the Student

A programed text is designed to induce you, the student, to take an active part in the learning process. As you use this book you will, in effect, reason your way through the program with the text serving as a tutor. The subject matter is organized into a series of segments called *frames*. Most frames require a written response which you are to supply after having read and concentrated upon the information given. A programed text allows you to check each response immediately, so that false concepts do not take root, and your attention is focused upon "right thinking." Since each frame builds upon the knowledge conveyed by previous ones, you must work your way through the program taking each frame in sequence. With a reasonable amount of concentration you should make few mistakes, for each successive step in the program is very small.

A glance at page 1 will show that it is divided into two parts. The correct answers appear on the left-hand side. These should be covered with a ruler or a slip of paper (merely the hand will do). Check your response to a given frame by uncovering the appropriate answer. *Your answer need not always be exactly the same as that supplied by the text.* Use your common sense to decide if it approximates the meaning of the one given. If you should make an excessive number of errors, repeat several of the preceding frames until your comprehension is improved. If this fails to remedy your difficulty, you should seek help from your instructor.

This text concentrates upon the *knowledge* of music fundamentals. Knowledge alone, however, is but one aspect of your musical development. In order to be useful, knowledge about music must be related to the actual experience of music as *sound*. Do not approach this study as merely the acquisition of knowledge; bring to bear your musical experiences as a performer and as a listener, and sing or play each item as it is presented. Only in this way will the relation of symbols to sounds become real and functional.

# Basic Materials in Music Theory

# 1
# The Basic Materials of Music: Time and Sound

The sensation of sound is produced by compression waves in the atmosphere emanating from a vibrating body. Because time is required for the transmission of even a single wave, sound cannot be experienced except within a period of time. Thus time and sound are the basic materials of music. It is the study of the characteristics of time and sound as well as their musical notation which shall concern us throughout this book. In this chapter you will learn about the properties of sound, and be introduced to some of the basic terminology used in the field of acoustics, the scientific study of sound.

| | |
|---|---|
| sound | 1. Sound is generated by a VIBRATING BODY such as a string, column of air, or metal plate. Any object which can be made to vibrate will produce sound, and music makes use of many kinds of sound sources. <br><br> A vibrating body is the source of _____ . |
| ear (or listener) | 2. Sound is transmitted to the ear by vibrational disturbance called SOUND WAVES. A simple sound wave is represented below: <br><br> One vibration <br><br> <br><br> Sound waves transmit energy from the vibrating body to the _____. |
| sound waves | 3. Sound waves are transmitted through the atmosphere as alternate compressions and rarefactions. These are received by the ear and produce in the listener the sensation of sound. <br><br> The atmosphere transmits vibrational disturbances called _____ _____. |

| | |
|---|---|
| ears | 4. Our perception of sound results from sound waves transmitted from the vibrating body to our _____. |
| "highness" (or) "lowness" | 5. Sounds impress us as being relatively "high" or "low." This property of sound is called PITCH. The pitch of a sound is determined by the FREQUENCY OF VIBRATION of the sound source.<br>     Pitch is a technical term which expresses the "_____ness" or "_____ness" of a sound. |
| pitch | 6. Frequency of vibration determines the _____ of a sound. |
| "lower" | 7. The faster the vibrating body is caused to vibrate, the "higher" the pitch. Conversely, the slower the vibrating body is caused to vibrate, the "_____" the pitch. |
| frequency | 8. The pitch of a sound is determined by the _____ of vibration. |
| pitch (or frequency) | 9. "High" and "low" are subjective descriptions of the _____ of a sound.<br><br>*Compare the effect of sounds produced by striking keys at the left end of the piano keyboard with those produced by striking keys at the right end.* |
| Higher. | 10. The terms <u>frequency</u> and <u>pitch</u> mean practically the same thing, and both are measured in terms of VIBRATIONS PER SECOND.<br>     Will a sound whose frequency is 1240 vibrations per second sound higher or lower than one whose frequency is 620 vibrations per second?<br>_____ |

lower

11. When the frequency of a pitch is <u>doubled</u>, the resulting tone will be an OCTAVE higher. When the frequency of a pitch is <u>halved</u>, the resulting tone will be an OCTAVE _____.

*Experience this effect at the piano by playing a note such as C or A in various octaves.*

---

12. Two simple sound waves are represented below:

(1)

(2)

Two vibrations of Wave 1 occur for each vibration of Wave 2. Thus Wave 1 represents a tone whose pitch is one octave (higher/lower) _____ than that of Wave 2.

higher

---

13. The tone whose frequency is 440 vibrations per second is called A. This tone is recognized in many countries as a standard of pitch.

The A an octave lower than this tone would vibrate at the rate of _____ vibrations per second.

220

| | |
|---|---|
| 522 | 14. The tone C has a frequency of 261 vibrations per second . The C an octave higher would vibrate at the rate of _____ vibrations per second. |
| lower | 15. A tone which has a frequency one-half that of another tone will be an octave (higher/lower) _____. |
| 1/4 | 16. The frequency of a tone two octaves lower than a second tone is (1/2, 1/3, 1/4, 1/8) _____ the frequency of the latter. |
| intensity | 17. The "loudness" or "softness" of a sound is known as INTENSITY. Intensity is determined by the amount of energy transmitted to the ear by the SOUND WAVE. The sound wave transmits not only pitch, but also _____. |
| Yes. | 18. Produce a relatively soft sound by humming or singing. Produce the same sound again but considerably louder.<br><br>Does the louder sound require a greater expenditure of energy? _____ |
| intensity | 19. Intensity is determined by the amount of energy transmitted from the sound source to the ear and is measured by the AMPLITUDE of the sound wave. Sound waves can be compared to waves on the surface of water: the greater the agitation the higher the waves. AMPLITUDE is a measurement of _____. |

20. Two simple sound waves are represented below:

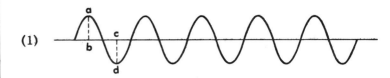

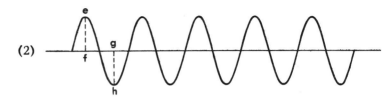

Lines a-b, c-d, e-f, and g-h show how amplitude is measured.

AMPLITUDE is a measurement of the disturbance caused by the sound waves. Which of the sounds represented above would be the louder? _____

(2).

---

"soft"

21. Sounds of high intensity impress us as being "loud," while sounds of low intensity impress us as being "_____."

---

lower (or weaker)

22. Intensity diminishes as sound travels through the atmosphere. The farther one is from the sound source, the _____ the intensity will be.

---

intensity

23. "Loud" and "soft" are subjective and relative terms. They refer to the _____ (technical term) of a sound.

---

higher (or stronger)

24. The nearer one is to a sound source, the _____ the intensity will be.

| | |
|---|---|
| timbre | 25. The ear is capable of distinguishing not only differences in PITCH and INTENSITY, but also differences in the "quality" of sounds. This property of sound is called TIMBRE. The property of sound which enables us to tell one musical instrument from another is called _____. |
| sound waves | 26. TIMBRE, as well as pitch and intensity, are transmitted to the ear by _____ _____. |
| (No response required.) | *Expository frame.*<br><br>27. Let us now consider what causes sounds from various sources to have their own distinctive <u>timbres</u>. There are several factors including the physical nature of the instrument, the acoustical characteristics of the place in which the sound is heard, and also the subjective response of the listener. Most important, though, is the fact that most sounds, instead of being a single tone, are composed of many pitches called PARTIALS. * The number, relative intensity, and distribution of the partials (harmonics) contained in a sound help determine its <u>timbre</u>. A sound with few audible partials has a "pure," "thin" quality, whereas one with many partials sounds "rich" and "full."<br><br>*The term <u>harmonics</u> is also used for these pitches. |
| partials | 28. The lowest partial is called the FUNDAMENTAL. The frequency of the fundamental of a tone is less than the frequency of any of the other _____. |
| True. | 29. The FUNDAMENTAL of a tone is one of the partials. (True/False) _____ |
| fundamental | 30. The partial with the lowest FREQUENCY is called the _____. |

| | |
|---|---|
| fundamental | 31. All partials other than the fundamental are called OVERTONES. All of the overtones plus the _____ constitute the entirety of the sound. |
| overtones | 32. In sounds produced by most of the instruments in common use, OVERTONES occur above a fundamental in a fixed order. This complex of pitches is called the NATURAL HARMONIC SERIES. The natural harmonic series consists of a fundamental plus all possible _____ . |
| Yes. | 33. Theoretically, the natural harmonic series extends indefinitely; but, for our purposes, the naming of eight partials will suffice. The series produced by the tone C is shown below. 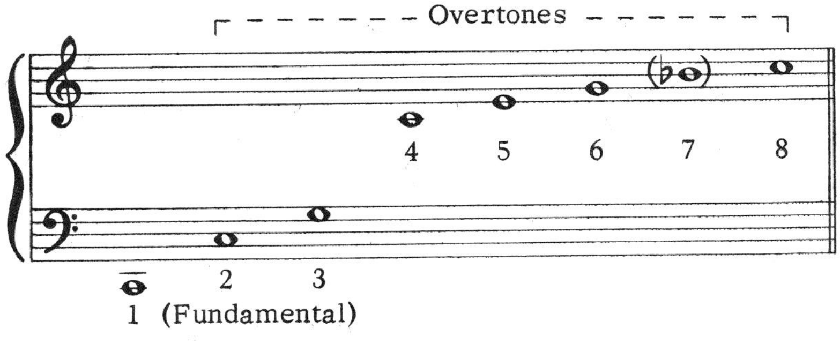<br><br><br><br>Notice that the partials numbered 2, 4, and 8 are octave duplications of the fundamental (1).<br><br>Is the first <u>overtone</u> the same tone as the second partial? _____ |

| | |
|---|---|
| fifth | 34. The natural harmonic series (shown in the preceding frame) is introduced here to help explain what causes different timbres, but it is also important in other areas of music study such as harmony and orchestration. Because you will make use of the natural harmonic series in future study, you should learn its structure and be able to play and write it on any pitch.<br><br>The fourth overtone is the same as the _____ partial. |
| Yes. | 35. The structure of the natural harmonic series is not influenced by the pitch of the fundamental; the same series of tones occurs over any pitch.<br><br>Is the fundamental considered one of the partials of a sound? _____ |
| partials | 36. The timbre of a sound is the result of the number, relative intensity, and distribution of the partials. Sounds vary in quality (timbre) due, in part, to differences in the intensity of their _____. |
| Timbre. | 37. What property of sound enables us to distinguish one sound source from another? _____ |
| False. | 38. Sounds produced by various sources vary greatly in the number and intensity of partials. Pure sounds (with no overtones) can be produced electronically, or by instruments such as the flute playing in the high register. Such sounds are relatively thin and colorless. Other instruments (the violin, oboe, and trumpet, to name a few) produce rich spectrums of partials, resulting in full, sonorous sounds.<br><br>All sound sources produce the same number of partials. (True/False) _____ |
| timbre | 39. The three properties of sound which have been examined to this point are pitch, intensity, and _____. |

| | |
|---|---|
| duration | 40. The fourth property of sound is DURATION. Since time is a basic material of music, duration of sound is an important factor.<br><br>Sounds not only have pitch, intensity, and timbre, but also _____. |
| rhythm | 41. The term RHYTHM applies to all aspects of time in music including duration. Music utilizes sounds ranging from very short to very long, and our system of notation is designed to indicate with precision the exact duration required.<br><br>All aspects of duration are part of the basic element of music called _____. |
| Time. | 42. Is rhythm primarily a matter of time or sound?<br>_____ |
| Your opinion. | 43. Can you conceive of rhythm without sound?<br>_____ |
| duration | 44. The property of sound which refers to the "length" of tones is called _____. |
| (1) pitch<br>(2) intensity<br>(3) timbre<br>*(Any order.)* | 45. The basic materials of music are TIME and SOUND. Durations of sounds are combined to produce <u>rhythm</u>. Duration is one of the properties of sound. Name the other three: (1) _____;<br>(2) _____; (3) _____. |

SUMMARY

There are four properties of sound, all of which are of vital concern for musicians. <u>Pitch</u> is the "highness" or "lowness" of sound and varies according to the frequency of vibration: higher frequencies produce higher pitches. Each time the frequency is doubled, the pitch is raised one octave. <u>Intensity</u> is the "loudness" or "softness" of a sound, and is the result of the amplitude of the sound wave. This in turn reflects the amount of energy emanating from the sound source. The "quality" of a sound is called <u>timbre</u> and results, in part, from the number, relative intensity, and distribution of the partials (harmonics) present. <u>Duration</u> is the fourth property of sound and is especially important for musicians because it is concerned with rhythm—one of the basic elements of music.

# 2
# The Notation of Pitch

The properties of sound presented in the preceding chapter (pitch, intensity, timbre, and duration) are indicated in music by various terms and systems of notation. In this chapter we shall study the notation of pitch. Because our system of notation originated many centuries ago when tonal materials were much simpler than now, it tends to be somewhat inadequate for the notation of modern, highly chromatic music. But, even though notation of pitch is unnecessarily complex, prevelant usage causes even minor changes to be adopted slowly. Modern notation is an imperfect, but nevertheless effective, visual representation of the "high" and "low" effects produced by tones of different pitch.

| | |
|---|---|
| pitch | 46. Five parallel horizontal lines with intervening spaces are used to notate the pitch of tones. This device is called a STAFF (pl. staves or staffs).<br><br>The staff is used to notate the property of sound called _____. |
| staff | 47. The five horizontal parallel lines with intervening spaces used for the notation of pitch are called the _____. |
| seen<br>(*The effect of a note can be imagined, but this is not an auditory sensation.*) | 48. The written symbols which represent tones are called NOTES. <u>Tones</u> can be heard, whereas <u>notes</u> can only be _____. |

| | |
|---|---|
| No.<br>*(It is the representation of a sound.)* | 49. A <u>tone</u> is a musical sound. Is a <u>note</u> also a sound? _____ |
| higher | 50. The lines and spaces of the staff are numbered from the bottom to the top.<br><br>LINES         SPACES<br><br>The fourth space is (higher/lower) _____ than the fourth line. |
| staff | 51. The first seven letters of the alphabet (A through G) are used to name the notes which are placed on the various lines and spaces of the staff.<br>    Signs are placed at the left on the staff to identify a particular line. These signs are called CLEFS.<br>    A <u>clef</u> sign is used to name a particular line of the _____. |
| (etc.) | 52. The modern clef signs are stylized forms of the Gothic letters G, F, and C. The TREBLE CLEF establishes the location of the note G on the second line of the staff.<br><br>G<br><br>Write several examples of the <u>treble</u> clef. |

53. By reference to the note established by the clef, the location of other notes can be established.

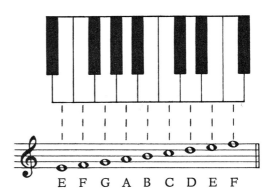

Since the lines and spaces represent an alphabetical sequence, all notes follow automatically once one pitch is located by the clef.

The <u>treble</u> clef places the note G on the _____ line of the staff.

second

---

54. Write the name of each note.

C, G, A, E, F, E, D

---

55. The BASS CLEF establishes the location of the note F on the fourth line of the staff.

The bass clef identifies the fourth line of the staff as _____.

F

𝄢 𝄢 𝄢 (etc.)

**56.** Write several examples of the <u>bass</u> clef.

---

fourth

**57.** The note F is located on the _____ line of the staff when the bass clef is used.

---

**58.** By reference to the note established by the clef, the location of the remaining notes can be established.

G  A  B  C  D  E  F  G  A

The bass clef identifies the third space as _____.

E

---

**59.** Write the name of each note.

D, A, G, E, F, G, C

—    —    —    —    —    —    —

---

**60.** The letter names of the lines and spaces of the staff change according to the clef. Whereas the second line of the staff is G when the TREBLE CLEF is used, the second line is _____ when the BASS CLEF is used.

B

61. Write the name of each note.

C, E, G, A, F, E

62. The C-CLEF establishes the location of the note C.*

The line which passes through the center of the C-CLEF is _____.

C

*This note is actually "middle C." The precise meaning of this term is explained later in this chapter. (See Frames 78-79.)

63. The C-CLEF can be placed on various lines of the staff.

TENOR CLEF (4th line)

ALTO CLEF (3rd line)

MEZZO-SOPRANO CLEF (2nd line)

SOPRANO CLEF (1st line)

The C-clef is not always located on the same line, but in each case the line which passes through the center of the clef is _____.

C

64. In modern notation, the alto clef is used by the viola, and the tenor clef is used by the 'cello, trombone, and bassoon. Other C-clefs are found mainly in older editions of choral music and are seldom used today. The C-clefs are introduced here to enable you to interpret them if necessary. (Only the treble and bass clefs are used in later chapters of this book.)

Write several examples of the alto clef.

---

The third.

65. On which line of the staff does the note C occur when the alto clef is used? _____

---

66. Write the name of each note.

B, E, G, F, A, G, D

— — — — — — —

---

The fourth.

67. Write several examples of the tenor clef.

---

68. On which line of the staff does the note C occur when the tenor clef is used? _____

---

G, E, C, A, D, E, B

69. Write the name of each note.

— — — — — — —

| | |
|---|---|
| bass | 70. The three clefs used in modern music notation are the C-clef, the treble clef, and the _____ clef. |
| staff | 71. The range of a staff may be extended by the use of LEDGER LINES. * These lines are added above or below a staff, and are spaced the same as the lines of the staff itself. The alphabetical succession of notes continues as on the staff.<br><br>    LEDGER LINES are used to extend the range of the _____ .<br><br>*The spelling <u>leger lines</u> is also used. |
| C | 72. Extension of the staff by means of ledger lines is shown below:<br><br><br><br>    The note on the second ledger line above the staff when the <u>treble</u> clef is used is _____ . |
| D | 73. Extension of the staff by means of ledger lines is shown below:<br><br><br><br>    The note on the second space below the staff when the <u>bass</u> clef is used is _____ . |

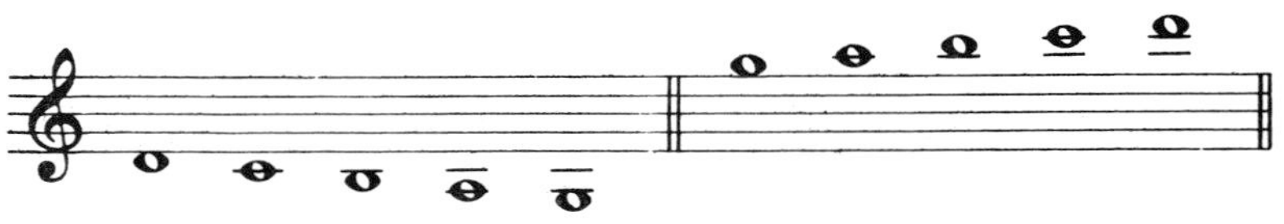

74. Write the name of each note.

(1) A, C, B, G, D
(2) G, D, B, A, C

75. Write the name of each note.

(1) D, B, C, F, E
(2) C, B, E, F, D

76. Write the name of each note.

B, C, C, B, D, A

77. Write the name of each note.

A, B, C, D, B, C

78. The treble and bass clefs are placed upon two staves joined by a vertical line and a brace at the left to form the GRAND STAFF.

The GRAND STAFF is used for the notation of piano music, and is useful for other purposes, since it is capable of representing the full range of virtually all musical media. The grand staff employs the _____ clef and the _____ clef.

treble-bass
(Any order.)

79. A note placed on the first ledger line above the bass staff represents the same pitch as a note placed on the first ledger line below the treble staff. This note is called MIDDLE C.

middle C

MIDDLE C derives its name from the fact that it is located in the middle of the _____ staff.

*This note is also approximately in the middle of the piano keyboard. Locate this note at the piano.*

grand

80. Other notes in addition to middle C can be notated on either the treble staff or the bass staff.
    Rewrite the notes on the bass staff so they will <u>sound</u> <u>the</u> <u>same</u>.

81. Rewrite the notes on the treble staff so they will <u>sound</u> <u>the</u> <u>same</u>.

82. Rewrite the notes on the alto staff so they will <u>sound</u> <u>the</u> <u>same</u>.

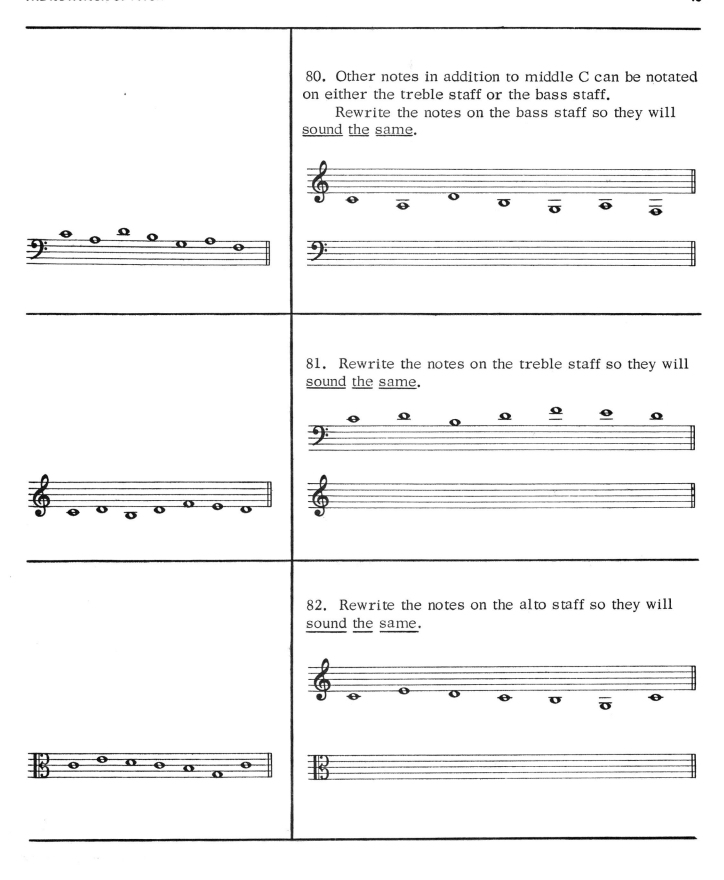

83. Rewrite the notes on the bass staff so they will sound the same.

84. Rewrite the notes on the tenor staff so they will sound the same.

85. Rewrite the notes on the treble staff so they will sound the same.

ledger lines

86. It is impractical to use more than three or four ledger lines, since notes become more difficult to read as the number of ledger lines increases. In order to avoid the excessive use of ledger lines, the treble staff may be extended upward and the bass staff extended downward by the use of the <u>ottava</u> sign ( *8 − − ⌐* , *8va − − ⌐* , or sometimes *8ve − − − ⌐* ).* Notes over which the <u>ottava</u> sign is placed sound an octave higher than written; notes below which the <u>ottava</u> sign is placed sound an octave lower than written.

     The <u>ottava</u> sign is used to avoid the excessive use of _____  _____.

*Recent practice gives preference to *8 ⁻ ⁻ ⌐* .

higher

87. Observe the use of the <u>ottava</u> sign below:

WRITTEN

SOUNDS

     The dotted line following the *8* indicates the notes affected by the sign.

     All notes over which the <u>ottava</u> sign appears are to be played an octave _____.

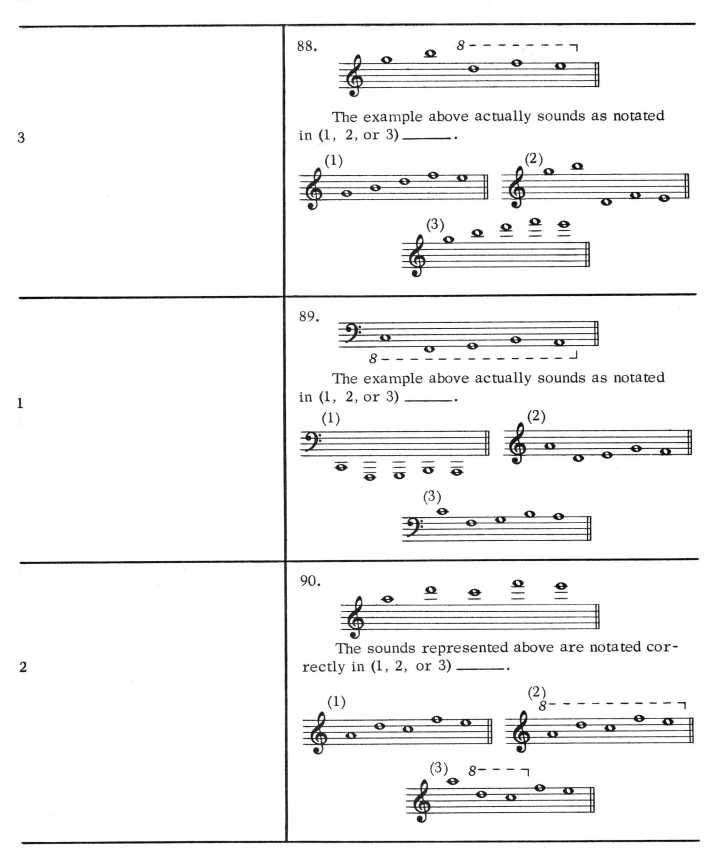

88.

The example above actually sounds as notated in (1, 2, or 3) _____.

3

(1)

(2)

(3)

89.

The example above actually sounds as notated in (1, 2, or 3) _____.

1

(1)

(2)

(3)

90.

The sounds represented above are notated correctly in (1, 2, or 3) _____.

2

(1)

(2)

(3)

91. Rewrite the passage below so it will <u>sound</u> <u>the same</u>, avoiding all use of ledger lines. *(Use the ottava sign.)*

92. Rewrite the passage below so it will <u>sound</u> <u>the same</u>. Use the <u>ottava</u> sign only for those notes which lie below the staff.

True.

93. Each note as written below notates the <u>same</u> <u>pitch</u>. (True/False) _____

True.

94. Each note as written below notates the <u>same</u> <u>pitch</u>. (True/False) _____

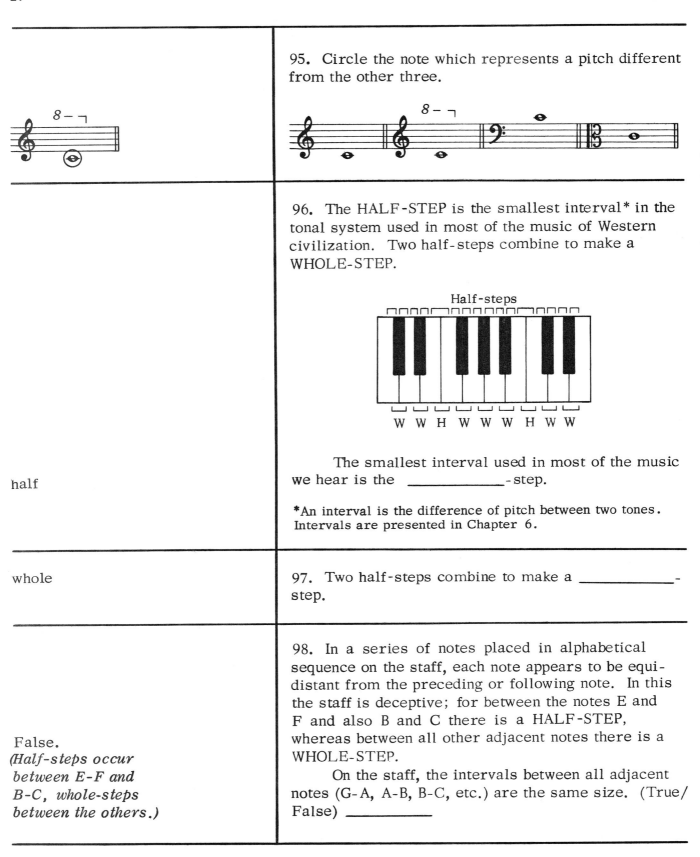

**95.** Circle the note which represents a pitch different from the other three.

half

**96.** The HALF-STEP is the smallest interval* in the tonal system used in most of the music of Western civilization. Two half-steps combine to make a WHOLE-STEP.

Half-steps

W  W  H  W  W  W  H  W  W

The smallest interval used in most of the music we hear is the _____-step.

*An interval is the difference of pitch between two tones. Intervals are presented in Chapter 6.

whole

**97.** Two half-steps combine to make a _____-step.

False.
*(Half-steps occur between E-F and B-C, whole-steps between the others.)*

**98.** In a series of notes placed in alphabetical sequence on the staff, each note appears to be equidistant from the preceding or following note. In this the staff is deceptive; for between the notes E and F and also B and C there is a HALF-STEP, whereas between all other adjacent notes there is a WHOLE-STEP.

On the staff, the intervals between all adjacent notes (G-A, A-B, B-C, etc.) are the same size. (True/False) _____

| | |
|---|---|
| E - F<br>B - C | 99. On the staff, half-steps occur between the notes _____ and _____ , and the notes _____ and _____ . |
| whole | 100. When notes are placed on the staff in alphabetical sequence (either ascending or descending), the succession is said to be STEPWISE or DIATONIC.<br><br>    In a STEPWISE (or DIATONIC) succession of notes (unaffected by accidentals), some intervals will be half-steps and some will be _____-steps. |
| half | 101. The interval between E and F is a _____-step. |
| whole | 102. The interval between A and B is a _____-step. |
| half | 103. The interval between B and C is a _____-step. |
| whole | 104. The interval between F and G is a _____-step. |
| whole | 105. The interval between G and A is a _____-step. |
| False.<br>*(It is a whole-step.)* | 106. The interval between C and D is a half-step. (True/False) _____ |
| True. | 107. The interval between D and E is a whole-step. (True/False) _____ |

stepwise (or diatonic)

108. When a succession of notes proceeds alpha-betically (either ascending or descending), the movement is said to be _____.

Yes.
(*All are whole-steps.*)

109. Do all the intervals below sound the same?
_____

110. Indicate where the half-steps occur. (*Use the sign* ∧ *between the proper notes.*)

111. Indicate where the half-steps occur. (*Use the sign* ∧ *between the proper notes.*)

112. Indicate where the half-steps occur. (*Use the sign* ∧ *between the proper notes.*)

113. Indicate where the half-steps occur. (*Use the sign* ∧ *between the proper notes.*)

Seven.
*(These are: A, B, C, D, E, F, and G.)*

**114.** All notes to this point have been BASIC NOTES. *
The term <u>basic</u> refers to notes which are not affected by certain signs called ACCIDENTALS.

How many basic notes occur in our system of notation? _____

*The term <u>basic</u> will be used later in connection with scales, intervals, and triads consisting of basic (unaltered) notes.

---

basic

**115.** The notes A, B, C, D, E, F, and G are called _____ notes.

---

**116.** Basic notes are altered by the use of signs called ACCIDENTALS, which are shown below.

| Sharp | ♯ | Double-sharp | 𝄪 |
| Flat | ♭ | Double-flat | 𝄫 |
| Natural | ♮ | | |

The SHARP ( ♯ ) raises the pitch of a note a half-step.

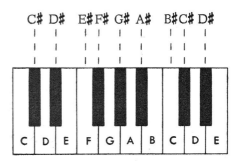

Apply a sharp to each note below. *(All accidentals are placed to the left of the note they are to affect.)*

117. The DOUBLE - SHARP ( ✖ ) raises a basic note <u>two</u> half-steps.

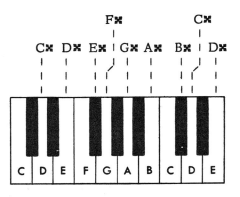

Apply a double-sharp to each note.

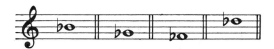

118. The FLAT ( ♭ ) lowers the pitch of a basic note a half-step.

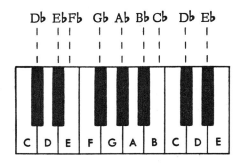

Apply a flat to each note.

**119.** The DOUBLE-FLAT ( 𝄫 ) lowers the pitch of a basic note <u>two</u> half-steps.

Apply a double-flat to each note.

**120.** The NATURAL ( ♮ ) cancels a previous accidental. *(The result is a basic note.)*
Apply a natural to the <u>second</u> note in each case.

half

**121.** The SHARP (♯) raises the pitch of a basic note by the interval of a _____-step.

half

**122.** The FLAT (♭) lowers the pitch of a basic note by the interval of a _____-step.

True.

**123.** The NATURAL (♮) has no effect upon a basic note unless it previously has been affected by another accidental or by a sharp or flat in the key signature. (True/False) _____

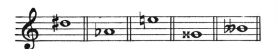

*(In all answers such as this the note may be written an octave higher or lower than shown.)*

**124.** Notes affected by accidentals are called A-flat, D-sharp, D-double-flat, G-sharp, E-natural, and so on.

Write the notes as directed. *(Remember: the accidental is placed to the left of the note it is to affect.)*

**125.** Vertical lines drawn through the five lines of the staff are called BAR LINES. These lines divide the music into MEASURES.

Accidentals remain in effect throughout the measure in which they occur; but they are cancelled by a bar line.

If an accidental is to be cancelled <u>within</u> a measure, what sign is used? _____

The natural (♮).

| | |
|---|---|
| | 126. The TIE is a curved line which connects two notes of the same pitch. It is used to prolong the duration of a note.<br><br>When a note which has been affected by an accidental is tied across a bar line, the accidental remains in effect for the duration of the tied note. |
| | <br>(B♭) ———————— (B♮) |
| tied | Accidentals remain in effect during the measure in which they occur, or when the altered note is _____ across a bar line. |
| bar | 127. Accidentals other than the sharps or flats of the key signature* are cancelled automatically by the _____ line.<br><br>*The key signature consists of a group of sharps or flats placed immediately after the clef sign on each line of music. A B-flat in the key signature causes all B's in the composition to be lowered to B-flat. Key signatures are studied in detail in Chapter 10. |
| tie | 128. An altered note may be prolonged into the next measure by means of the _____. |
| The second. | 129. If a double-sharp is to be converted later in the same measure to a sharp, a natural sign is sometimes used to cancel the double-sharp, and the desired accidental is then applied.*<br><br>This practice does not apply to the double-flat.<br><br>If a natural plus a sharp appears before a note, which accidental actually applies? (The first/The second) _____<br><br>*This practice is rarely observed today. Only the desired accidental is used, the natural being omitted as superfluous. |

130. Accidentals are usually interpreted as affecting only notes on the particular line or space on which they are written, not notes in other octaves.

Since no sharp appears on the fourth line in the example above, the third note should be played as a D-natural.

G-natural.

What is the pitch of the fifth note? _____

131. Write the name of each note. (*Use signs such as* A♯, F♮, *etc.*)

E♭, C♯, G♮, B♭♭, D♯

___   ___   ___   ___   ___

132. When accidentals are applied so that two or more basic notes represent the <u>same</u> <u>pitch</u> these notes are said to be ENHARMONIC. Enharmonic notes are written differently but have the same

pitch

_____ .

133. Examples of ENHARMONIC notes are shown below.

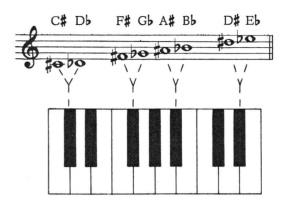

Two basic notes a whole-step apart can be made enharmonic by applying a flat to the upper note and a _____ to the lower.

sharp

134. Other examples of ENHARMONIC notes are shown below.

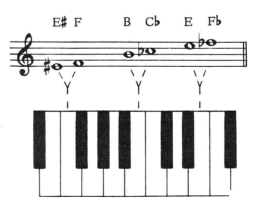

Two basic notes separated by a half-step can be made enharmonic either by raising the lower note a half-step or by _____ the upper note a half-step.

lowering

135. Still other examples of ENHARMONIC notes are shown below.

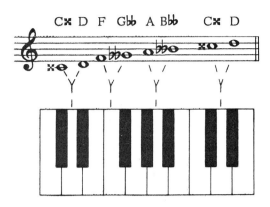

Write the two accidentals which are capable of altering the pitch of a tone by the interval of a whole-step. _____ _____

x    bb

136. Three basic notes can be made enharmonic, as is shown below.

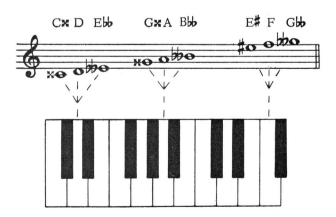

Notes which sound the same but are written differently are said to be _____.

enharmonic

(1) B♯ or D♭♭
(2) D𝄪 or F♭
(3) A♭

137. Write an enharmonic equivalent for each note.

(1) C♯ or B𝄪
(2) C♭ or A𝄪
(3) A♭♭ or F𝄪

138. Write an enharmonic equivalent for each note.

139. Half-steps occur naturally between the notes E and F and the notes B and C. By the use of accidentals, half-steps can be written between other notes as well.

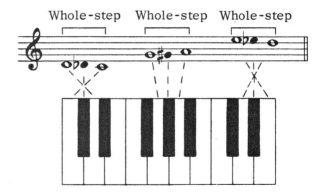

Successions of notes moving exclusively in half-steps are said to be CHROMATIC. A chromatic succession of notes moves entirely in _____-steps.

half

**140.** Distinction is made between DIATONIC and CHROMATIC half-steps. A <u>diatonic</u> half-step uses two basic notes, while a <u>chromatic</u> half-step uses only one.

DIATONIC HALF-STEPS          CHROMATIC HALF-STEPS

Is the interval D up to D-sharp a <u>diatonic</u> or a <u>chromatic</u> half-step? _____

Chromatic.

---

Diatonic.

**141.** Is the interval D up to E-flat a <u>diatonic</u> or a <u>chromatic</u> half-step? _____

---

**142.** Write a <u>diatonic</u> half-step above F.

---

**143.** Write a <u>chromatic</u> half-step above F.

half

B-C   E-F

**144.** Below is an example of a CHROMATIC SCALE. *

The notation of chromatic scales may vary according to the keys in which they occur. The simplest notation, however, results if sharps are used for notes inflected upward and flats are used for notes inflected downward. Observe in the example above that E and B are the only basic notes which are unaffected by accidentals. This is because the intervals between E and F and between B and C are _____ steps.

*A scale consists of the tones contained in one octave arranged in consecutive series. Scales are studied in detail in Chapters 7, 8, and 9.

**145.** Below is another example of a CHROMATIC SCALE.

Flats are usually used for notes inflected downward. Observe that F and C are the only basic notes unaffected by accidentals. This is due to the fact that there is a half-step between the notes _____ and _____, and the notes _____ and _____.

**146.** Write a CHROMATIC SCALE ascending from C to C. (Use only sharps.)

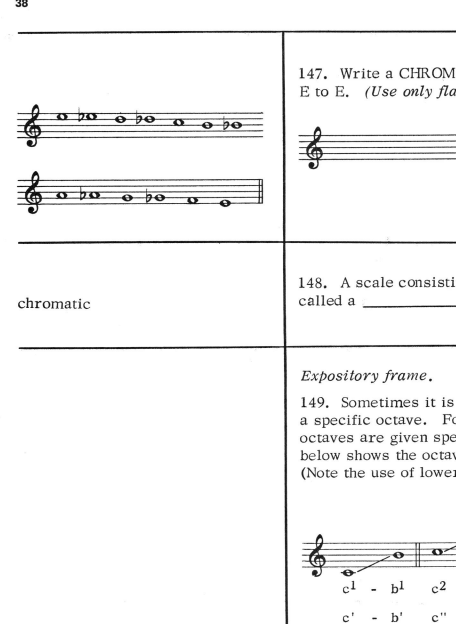

**147.** Write a CHROMATIC SCALE descending from E to E. *(Use only flats.)*

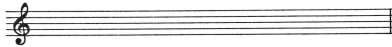

---

chromatic

**148.** A scale consisting entirely of half-steps is called a _____ scale.

---

*Expository frame.*

**149.** Sometimes it is necessary to refer to a note in a specific octave. For this purpose, the various octaves are given special designations.* The example below shows the octaves upward from middle C. (Note the use of lowercase letters.)

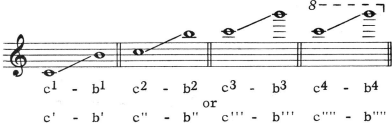

All of the notes from middle C up to and including the next B are included in the one-line octave. For higher octaves, the terms two-line octave, three-line octave, and four-line octave are used. You may refer to a note such as $g^2$ as either "two-line g" or "g two."

*Unfortunately, octave designations are not standardized; so you must be alert to the terms and symbols used by other writers.

*(No response required.)*

**150.** Indicate the octave into which each note falls. *(Use the terms one-line, two-line, etc.)*

(1) two-line
(2) three-line
(3) one-line

(1) _____ octave
(2) _____ octave
(3) _____ octave

**151.** Write the notes as indicated. *(Use the ottava sign to avoid excessive ledger lines.)*

(1) a³   (2) bb¹   (3) f#²

**152.** Continue as in the preceding frame.

(1) c#⁴   (2) g#²   (3) d¹

True.

**153.** The one-line octave begins on middle C. (True/False) _____

**154.** The first two octaves below middle C are shown below:

b  -  c    B  -  C

The first octave below middle C is called the <u>small octave</u>, and lowercase letters are used; the second is called the <u>great octave</u>, and capital letters are used.

The note great A is _____ octaves below a¹.

two

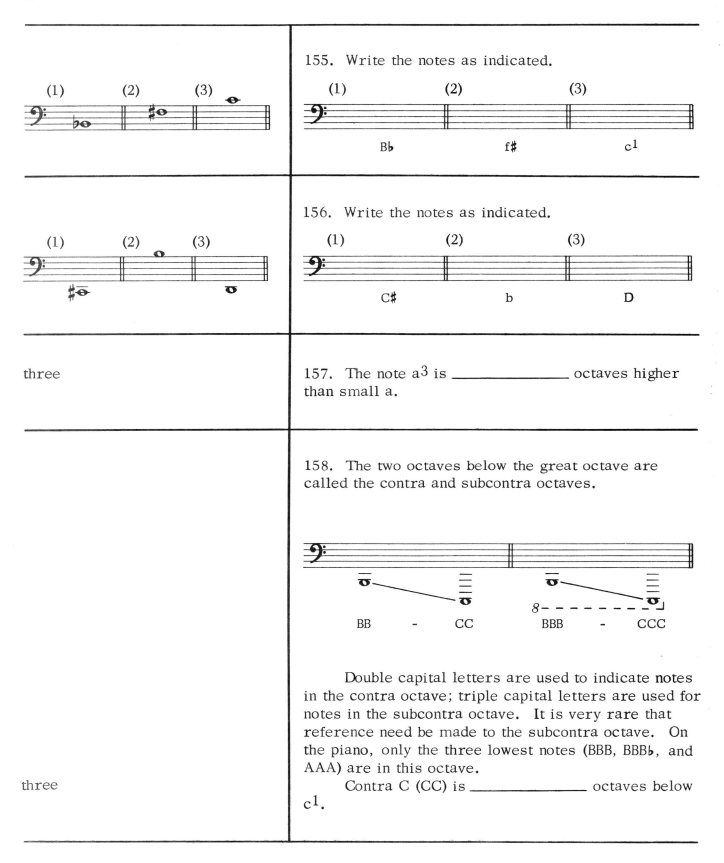

**155.** Write the notes as indicated.

(1)                    (2)                    (3)

Bb                     f♯                     c¹

**156.** Write the notes as indicated.

(1)                    (2)                    (3)

C♯                     b                      D

three

**157.** The note a³ is _____ octaves higher than small a.

**158.** The two octaves below the great octave are called the contra and subcontra octaves.

BB    -    CC         BBB    -    CCC

Double capital letters are used to indicate notes in the contra octave; triple capital letters are used for notes in the subcontra octave. It is very rare that reference need be made to the subcontra octave. On the piano, only the three lowest notes (BBB, BBBb, and AAA) are in this octave.
        Contra C (CC) is _____ octaves below c¹.

three

159. Write the notes as indicated. *(Use the ottava sign to avoid excessive ledger lines.)*

(1)　　　　(2)　　　　(3)

FF　　　　GGG　　　　AAb

160. Continue as in the preceding frame.

(1)　　　　(2)　　　　(3)

Db　　　　DDb　　　　db

161. The example below shows the lower note of each octave with its symbol.

CCC　CC　C　c　$c^1$　$c^2$　$c^3$　$c^4$

How many octaves higher is $c^3$ than CC?

_____

Five.

## SUMMARY

Many special symbols are required for the specific representation of pitches. Not only is the meaning of the staff modified by the use of various clef signs, but also the basic notes are inflected either upward or downward a half-step by the use of sharps and flats. In addition to these, double sharps and double flats, which alter the pitch of a basic note a whole-step, as well as natural signs are necessary for correct notation. Ledger lines extend the range of the staff both upward and downward. The ottava sign is used to avoid excessive ledger lines.

# 3
# Time Classification

In this chapter we shall see how time is organized for musical purposes; later, the notation of rhythm will be presented. The simplest organization of time is by the establishment of a regular series of pulsations. These pulsations are called beats, and they are the foundation on which the whole rhythmic structure is built. Beats of unequal duration are possible, and frequently are exploited by twentieth-century composers. Most music of the eighteenth and nineteenth centuries, however, utilizes regular beats. Because of the fundamental nature of this book, this study of rhythm is limited to the practices of traditional music.

| | |
|---|---|
| stress | 162. In most music, pulsations called BEATS divide time into regular units of duration. Beats themselves have little expressive value, but additional interest results if some are stressed more strongly than others.<br><br>Beats may vary in the degree of _____. |
| No. | 163. The principle of tension and relaxation is brought into play when beats are given varying degrees of stress. Does the degree of stress affect the duration of the beat? _____ |
| stress | 164. Patterns of stress are known as METER. Meter is the pattern produced by beats of varying degrees of _____. |
| meter | 165. The pattern which results from beats of varying degrees of stress is called the _____. |

beats

166.  Stressed beats are called STRONG; unstressed beats are called WEAK.  The meter results from patterns of strong and weak _____.

---

167.  The simplest pattern of stresses possible is an alternation of strong and weak beats.

STRESS PATTERNS:  > ∪  > ∪  > ∪

BEATS:  1  2  1  2  1  2

> = a strong beat
∪ = a weak beat

Since each pattern ( > ∪ ) consists of two beats, the term DUPLE METER is used.  In a DUPLE pattern the beat is organized into a sequence of one strong and one _____ pulsation.

*Tap this pattern and stress each first beat as indicated. Notice your response to this meter.*

weak

---

duple

168.  The simplest possible pattern of stresses results from an alternation of strong and weak beats.  This pattern is called _____ meter.

triple

169. Another simple pattern results when every third pulse is stressed.

STRESS PATTERNS: ⟩  ᴜ  ᴜ    ⟩  ᴜ  ᴜ

BEATS:  1   2   3    1   2   3

Since each pattern ( ⟩ ᴜ ᴜ ) consists of three beats, the term TRIPLE METER is used. A strong-weak-weak succession of pulsations results in an organization known as _____ meter.

*Tap this pattern and stress each first beat as indicated. Compare the effect of this meter with that of the meter discussed in Frame 167.*

two

170. In TRIPLE METER the beat is organized into a sequence of one strong and _____ weak beats.

Duple: ⟩ ᴜ (etc.)
Triple: ⟩ ᴜ ᴜ  (etc.)

171. Indicate the patterns of pulsations for <u>duple</u> and <u>triple</u> meter. *(Use the signs ⟩ and ᴜ.)*

Duple meter: _____
Triple meter: _____

strong-weak-weak

172. DUPLE METER and TRIPLE METER are the two fundamental patterns produced by beats of varying degrees of stress. Duple meter is a succession of strong-weak beats; triple meter is a series of _____ - _____ - _____ beats.

173. Other more complex patterns result from combinations of duple and triple patterns. QUADRUPLE METER is a combination of two duple patterns in which the first beat is stressed more strongly than the third.

```
┌──────────────── QUADRUPLE METER ────────────────┐
┌ ─ ─ ─ Duple ─ ─ ─ ┐ ┌ ─ ─ ─ Duple ─ ─ ─ ┐
>              U              >              U
1              2              3              4
```

duple

A four-beat pattern results from a combination of two _____ patterns.

The first.

174. In QUADRUPLE METER both the first and third beats are strong. Which, however, is the stronger? _____

quadruple

175. A combination of two duple patterns results in _____ meter.

Two (and) four

176. Which are the weak beats in quadruple meter? _____ and _____ .

Two (and) three

177. Which are the weak beats in triple meter? _____ and _____ .

**178.** A five-beat pattern is called QUINTUPLE METER. This results from a combination of a duple and a triple pattern.

```
┌──────────────── QUINTUPLE METER ────────────────┐
│                                                  │
┌─ ─ ─ Duple ─ ─ ─┐  ┌─ ─ ─ ─ ─Triple ─ ─ ─ ─ ─┐
>         ∪          >         ∪         ∪
1         2          3         4         5
```

or

```
┌──────────────── QUINTUPLE METER ────────────────┐
│                                                  │
┌─ ─ ─ ─ ─Triple ─ ─ ─ ─ ─┐  ┌─ ─ ─Duple ─ ─ ─┐
>         ∪         ∪          >         ∪
1         2         3          4         5
```

Either the duple or the triple pattern may come first; but in either case, the first stressed beat (1) is the strongest.

A five-beat pattern results when a duple and a _____ pattern are combined.

triple

---

**179.** A pattern of >∪>∪∪ or >∪∪>∪ is called _____ meter.

quintuple

---

**180.** There are three strong beats in quintuple meter. (True/False) _____

False.
*(There are two strong beats.)*

---

**181.** How many weak beats occur in quintuple meter?

_____

Three.

---

**182.** QUINTUPLE METER is a combination of a triple pattern and a _____ pattern.

duple

> ∪ > ∪ ∪ or
> ∪ ∪ > ∪

183. Indicate the pattern of beats known as quintuple meter. *(Use the signs > and ∪.)*

_____

(1) Duple
(2) triple
*(Any order.)*

184. The process of combining duple and triple stress patterns can be carried on to include six-beat patterns, seven-beat patterns, and so forth; but in actual musical experiences, the ear tends to reject the larger patterns and focus instead upon smaller organizations. Thus a six-beat pattern would probably be heard as a combination of two three-beat patterns, and a seven-beat pattern as a combination of a four-beat plus a three-beat pattern (or the reverse).

What are the two basic meters which are combined to produce more complex ones? (1) _____; and (2) _____ .

quadruple

185. The stress pattern (> ∪ > ∪ ) is called _____ meter.

duple

186. The stress pattern (> ∪ ) is called _____ meter.

triple

187. The stress pattern (> ∪ ∪ ) is called _____ meter.

beats

188. The terms DUPLE, TRIPLE, QUADRUPLE, and QUINTUPLE refer to the number of _____ in each stress pattern.

---

Three.

189. Each stress pattern constitutes a MEASURE. A measure in triple meter consists of how many beats? _____

---

beats

190. MEASURES vary in length according to the number of _____ in each stress pattern.

---

subdivided

191. The rhythmic interest of a composition would be slight indeed if the duration of all tones should coincide with the beat. Actually, a single beat may contain two, three, four, five, or more tones. Thus beats are <u>divided</u> normally into two or three parts, or <u>subdivided</u> normally into four or six parts. *

The beat itself is the most elementary organization of time possible. By establishing a meter through patterns of stress the musical value of the beat is increased. A higher level of rhythmic complexity results from dividing the beat into two or three equal parts. Still greater rhythmic interest is obtained if the beat is _____ into four or six parts.

*Irregular groups of notes are presented in Chapter 4, Frames 308-312.

| | |
|---|---|
| beats | 192. We shall now concentrate on two basic types of rhythmic organization which are determined by how beats are normally divided.<br><br>If beats are divided consistently into <u>two</u> equal parts, the term SIMPLE TIME is used; if beats are divided consistently into <u>three</u> equal parts, the term COMPOUND TIME is used.<br><br>The terms SIMPLE TIME and COMPOUND TIME refer to the manner in which _____ are divided. |
| Two. | 193. In SIMPLE TIME beats are divided normally into how many equal parts? _____ |
| compound | 194. If beats are divided consistently into <u>three</u> equal parts, the term _____ time is used. |
| two (or) three | 195. Beats may be divided into either _____ or _____ equal parts. |
| divided | 196. The terms <u>duple</u>, <u>triple</u>, <u>quadruple</u>, and <u>quintuple</u> refer to the number of beats per measure, whereas the terms <u>simple</u> and <u>compound</u> refer to the manner in which beats normally are _____ . |

197.  A TIME CLASSIFICATION identifies the organization of the meter and indicates the <u>normal</u> <u>division</u>
<u>of</u> <u>the</u> <u>beat</u>.

In DUPLE METER the stress pattern consists
of two beats ( > ⌣ ).  If each beat is divided into <u>two</u>
equal parts, the time classification is DUPLE-SIMPLE.

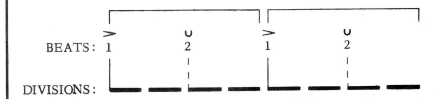

The term <u>duple-simple</u> means there are two
beats per measure, and each beat is divided into
_____ equal parts.

two

198.  If the beats in DUPLE METER are divided into
<u>three</u> equal parts, the time classification is DUPLE-
COMPOUND.

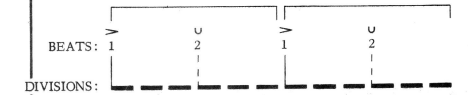

The term <u>duple-compound</u> means there are
two beats per measure, and each beat is divided
into _____ equal parts.

three

two

199. The term SIMPLE TIME means that beats are normally divided into _____ equal parts.

three

200. The term COMPOUND TIME means that beats are normally divided into _____ equal parts.

201. Music in simple time affects us quite differently than does music in compound time.

Sing the song "Yankee Doodle" as notated below:

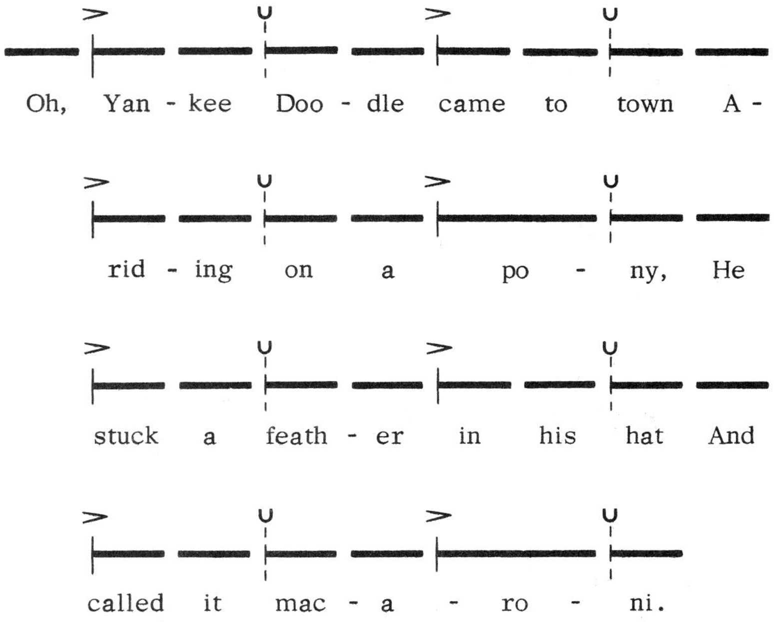

> Oh, Yan - kee Doo - dle came to town A -

rid - ing on a po - ny, He

stuck a feath - er in his hat And

called it mac - a - ro - ni.

Since the beats are divided consistently into <u>two</u> equal parts, this is an example of duple-_____ time.

simple

202. Sing the song "Three Blind Mice" as notated below:

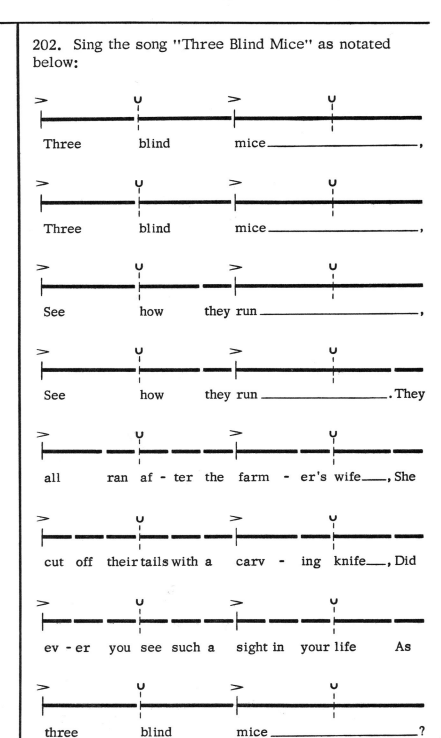

compound

This song is an example of duple-_____ time.

Your opinion.

203. Composers often use simple time to express musical ideas which are "strong," "straightforward," or "positive"; while compound time is often used for ideas of a more "flowing" or "swaying" nature. Do you think the songs in Frames 201 and 202 demonstrate these characteristics? _____

Your opinion.

204. Do you think simple and compound time need <u>always</u> give rise to emotional responses such as these? _____

beat

205. Time classifications are interpreted as follows: The <u>first</u> part of the classification refers to the number of beats per measure; the <u>second</u> part indicates the manner in which beats are normally divided.

　　Thus the time classification DUPLE-SIMPLE means that there are two beats per measure and the normal division of the beat is into two equal parts.

　　Time classifications indicate not only the number of beats per measure, but also the normal division of the _____.

three

206. Duple-simple and duple-compound time both have two beats per measure; but in duple-<u>simple</u> time the beat is divided into two equal parts, while in duple-<u>compound</u> time the beat is divided into _____ equal parts.

| | |
|---|---|
| The number of beats per measure. | 207. What does the <u>first</u> part of a time classification indicate? _____ |
| The normal division of the beat. | 208. What does the <u>second</u> part of a time classifica- tion indicate? _____ |
| two | 209. TRIPLE-SIMPLE indicates: (1) three beats per measure; and (2) the division of each beat into _____ equal parts. |
| four | 210. QUADRUPLE-COMPOUND indicates: (1) _____ beats per measure; and (2) the division of each beat into three equal parts. |
| three | 211. TRIPLE-COMPOUND indicates: (1) three beats per measure; and (2) the division of each beat into _____ equal parts. |
| two | 212. QUADRUPLE-SIMPLE indicates: (1) four beats per measure; and (2) the division of each beat into _____ equal parts. |
| five | 213. QUINTUPLE-SIMPLE indicates: (1) _____ beats per measure; and (2) the division of each beat into two equal parts. |

| | |
|---|---|
| three | 214. DUPLE-COMPOUND indicates: (1) two beats per measure; and (2) the division of each beat into _____ equal parts. |
| two | 215. DUPLE-SIMPLE indicates: (1) two beats per measure; and (2) the division of each beat into _____ equal parts. |
| three | 216. QUINTUPLE-COMPOUND indicates: (1) five beats per measure; and (2) the division of each beat into _____ equal parts. |
| duple-simple | 217. If there are two beats per measure and each beat is divided into two equal parts, the time classification is _____ - _____ . |
| triple-simple | 218. If there are three beats per measure and each beat is divided into two equal parts, the time classification is _____ - _____ . |
| quadruple-compound | 219. If there are four beats per measure and each beat is divided into three equal parts, the time classification is_____ - _____ . |

| | |
|---|---|
| quintuple-simple | 220. If there are five beats per measure and each beat is divided into two equal parts, the time classification is _____-_____. |
| quintuple-compound | 221. If there are five beats per measure and the beat is divided into three equal parts, the time classification is _____-_____. |
| quadruple-simple | 222. If there are four beats per measure and each beat is divided into two equal parts, the time classification is _____-_____. |
| triple-compound | 223. If there are three beats per measure and each beat is divided into three equal parts, the time classification is _____-_____. |
| duple-compound | 224. If there are two beats per measure and each beat is divided into three equal parts, the time classification is _____-_____. |
| True. | 225. The terms duple, triple, quadruple, and quintuple refer to the number of beats per measure. (True/False) _____ |
| How each beat is divided. | 226. To what do the terms simple and compound refer? _____ |

| | |
|---|---|
| beat | **227.** The regularly recurring pulse of music is called the _____. |
| first | **228.** The number of beats per measure is expressed by the (first/second) _____ part of the time classification. |
| simple (and) compound | **229.** The beat can be divided into <u>two</u> or <u>three</u> equal parts. This division is expressed by the terms _____ and _____. |
| triplet | **230.** The natural division of the beat in <u>simple</u> time is into <u>two</u> equal parts. The division of the beat into <u>three</u> equal parts in simple time is called a BORROWED DIVISION (or <u>triplet</u>).<br><br>    Tap (or say with the syllable *ta*) the divisions expressed in line notation below:<br><br>SIMPLE TIME<br><br>BEAT: 1     2<br><br>DIVISION:<br><br>BORROWED DIVISION:<br><br>    The borrowed division in <u>simple</u> time is sometimes called a _____. |
| borrowed | **231.** "TRIPLET" is another name for a _____ division. |

232. The natural division of the beat in compound time is into three equal parts. The division of the beat into two equal parts in compound time is called a BORROWED DIVISION (or duplet).

Tap (or say with the syllable *ta*) the divisions expressed in line notation below:

COMPOUND TIME

| | | |
|---|---|---|
| | > | ∪ |
| BEAT: | 1 | 2 |

DIVISION: ▬ ▬ ▬ | ▬ ▬ ▬

BORROWED DIVISION: ▬ ▬ | ▬ ▬

The borrowed division in compound time is a division of the beat into _____ equal parts.

two

---

233. The term borrowed division refers to the use of a division in simple time which is normal in compound time or vice versa. The division is literally "borrowed" from one for use in the other.

The borrowed division in simple time is a division of the beat into _____ equal parts.

three

---

234. Is the division of the beat into TWO equal parts a natural division in simple time? _____

Yes.

---

235. Is the division of the beat into TWO equal parts a natural division in compound time? _____

No.
(*This is a borrowed division or duplet.*)

---

236. Is the division of the beat into THREE equal parts a natural division in simple time? _____

No.
(*This is a borrowed division or triplet.*)

| | |
|---|---|
| simple | 237. In SIMPLE TIME the beat <u>sub</u>divides into four equal parts. Four is the normal subdivision of the beat in _____ time. |
| compound | 238. In COMPOUND TIME the beat <u>sub</u>divides into six equal parts. Six is the normal subdivision of the beat in _____ time. |
| Four. | 239. What is the natural subdivision of the beat in <u>simple</u> time? _____ |
| Six. | 240. What is the natural subdivision of the beat in <u>compound</u> time? _____ |
| False. *(The term compound time refers to the division of the beat into three equal parts, not to the number of beats per measure.)* | 241. The term compound time means there are three beats per measure. (True/False) _____ |
| True. | 242. The term DUPLE refers to a meter which has two beats per measure. (True/False) _____ |

| | |
|---|---|
| 2. | 243. What is the natural division of the beat in <u>simple</u> time?  (2, 3, 4, 6) ____ |
| 3. | 244. What is the natural division of the beat in <u>compound</u> time?  (2, 3, 4, 6) _____ |
| 4. | 245. What is the natural subdivision of the beat in <u>simple</u> time? (2, 3, 4, 6) ____ |
| 6. | 246. What is the natural subdivision of the beat in <u>compound</u> time? (2, 3, 4, 6) ____ |
| 3. | 247. In simple time a BORROWED DIVISION divides the beat into how many parts? (2, 3, 4, 6) ___ |
| 2. | 248. In compound time a BORROWED DIVISION divides the beat into how many parts? (2, 3, 4, 6)___ |
| True. | 249. The TRIPLET is the same as a borrowed division in simple time. (True/False) _____ |
| True. | 250. The DUPLET is the same as a borrowed division in compound time. (True/False) _____ |

SUMMARY

Time is organized on various levels of complexity. The simplest is the series of pulsations called the beat. Next is meter, which results from patterns of stress imposed on the beat. The more common meters are duple, triple, quadruple, and quintuple depending on the number of beats between each primary stress. The next level of rhythmic organization is the result of dividing beats into either two or three parts. The term simple time refers to the division of the beat into two equal parts; the term compound time refers to the division of the beat into three equal parts. Borrowed divisions occur when the normal division in compound time is used in simple time, or vice versa. Beats subdivide normally into four parts in simple time, and six parts in compound time.

# 4
# Note and Rest Values

The symbols used to represent tones are called notes. In addition to identifying pitch, notes indicate relative duration. Although the rhythmic element of music can be quite complex, there are only a few basic types of notes, and these bear a simple relationship to one another: each is one-half the value of the next-greater note.

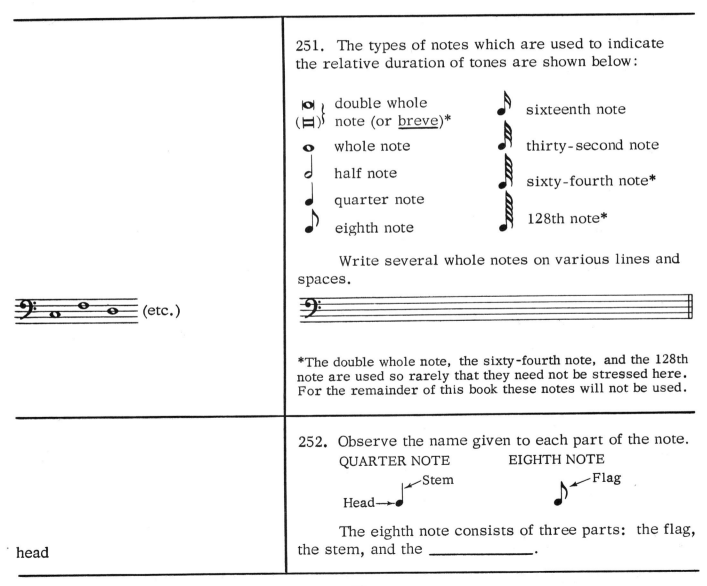

251. The types of notes which are used to indicate the relative duration of tones are shown below:

- double whole note (or breve)*
- whole note
- half note
- quarter note
- eighth note
- sixteenth note
- thirty-second note
- sixty-fourth note*
- 128th note*

Write several whole notes on various lines and spaces.

*The double whole note, the sixty-fourth note, and the 128th note are used so rarely that they need not be stressed here. For the remainder of this book these notes will not be used.

252. Observe the name given to each part of the note.

QUARTER NOTE
Head→ Stem

EIGHTH NOTE
Flag

The eighth note consists of three parts: the flag, the stem, and the _____.

head

62

right

253. Stems are one octave in length. They are placed on the right side of the head and extend upward if the note is below the third (middle) line of the staff.

If the note is below the third line of the staff, the stem is placed on the _____ side of the head.

---

third (or middle)

254. If the note is above the third line of the staff, the stem is placed on the left side of the head and extends downward.

Stems are placed on the left side of the head and extend downward if the note is above the _____ line of the staff.

---

right

255. If the note is on the third (middle) line of the staff, the stem may extend either upward or downward.*  If the stem extends downward it is placed on the left side of the head; if it extends upward it is placed on the right side of the head.

All stems which extend downward are placed on the left side of the head. All stems which extend upward are placed on the _____ side of the head.

*Most printed music shows a preference for the downward stem when notes are on the third line.

**256.** The flag appears on the right side of the stem in all cases.

Add a stem and one flag to each note head.

**257.** Add a stem and two flags to each note head.

sixteenth

**258.** The notes in the preceding frame are (half/quarter/eighth/sixteenth) _____ notes.

**259.** Circle the notes which are <u>not</u> correctly written.

(etc.)

**260.** Write several half notes on various lines and spaces. *(Observe correct placement of stems.)*

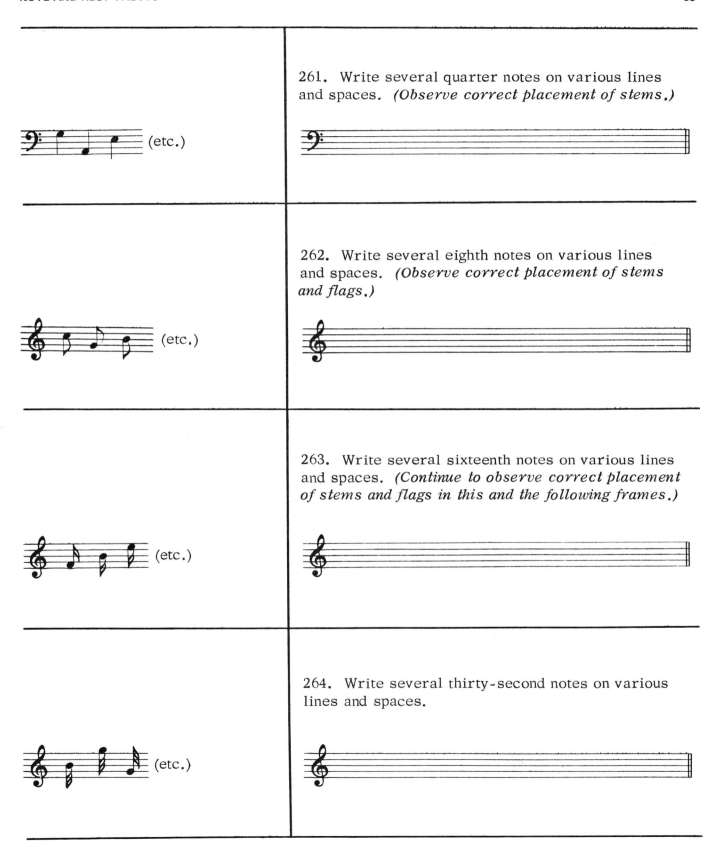

261. Write several quarter notes on various lines and spaces. *(Observe correct placement of stems.)*

262. Write several eighth notes on various lines and spaces. *(Observe correct placement of stems and flags.)*

263. Write several sixteenth notes on various lines and spaces. *(Continue to observe correct placement of stems and flags in this and the following frames.)*

264. Write several thirty-second notes on various lines and spaces.

265. Instead of a separate flag for each note, BEAMS are often used to join several notes together.

Beams generally connect notes which are to sound within the same metrical unit (the beat or measure).

Beams take the place of _____ .

flags

266. The use of beams often causes one or more of the stems to be placed differently than would be the case if a flag were used.  If most of the notes are above the third (middle) line of the staff, stems extend <u>downward</u>; if most of the notes are below the third line, the stems extend <u>upward</u>.

Note that beams are always <u>straight</u> lines.

Connect the notes in each group with beams as directed.

(1)   EIGHTH NOTES               (2)  SIXTEENTH NOTES

(1)

(2)

(1)

(2)

267. Continue as in the preceding frame.

(1) EIGHTH NOTES    (2) THIRTY-SECOND NOTES

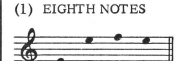 

268. If the number of notes above the middle line of the staff is equal to the number below, the direction of the stems is determined by the note which is <u>farthest</u> from the middle line.

Connect the notes in each group with beams as directed.

(1) SIXTEENTH NOTES    (2) SIXTY-FOURTH NOTES

(1)

(2)

269. Notes do not, in themselves, indicate duration precisely, but their values are related in the manner indicated by the name of each note.

A whole note = 2 half notes.
A whole note = 4 quarter notes.
A whole note = 8 eighth notes.
(etc. )

A whole note = how many sixteenth notes?

16.

_____

| | |
|---|---|
| four | **270.** Whereas two quarter notes equal one half note, it requires _____ eighth notes to equal one half note. |
| 2. | **271.** A quarter note equals how many eighth notes? _____ |
| 4. | **272.** A quarter note equals how many sixteenth notes? _____ |
| 2. | **273.** An eighth note equals how many sixteenth notes? _____ |
| (1) 2 <br> (2) 2 <br> (3) 2 | **274.** Supply the answer in each case. <br><br> (1) A o note = _____ ♩ notes. <br> (2) A ♩ note = _____ ♪ notes. <br> (3) A ♩ note = _____ ♪ notes. |

(1) 4

(2) 8

(3) 8

275. Continue as in the preceding frame.

(1) A 𝅝 note = _____ ♩ notes.

(2) A ♩ note = _____ ♫ notes.

(3) A ♩ note = _____ ♬ notes.

(1) 2

(2) 2

(3) 4

276. Continue as in the preceding frame.

(1) An ♪ note = _____ ♫ notes.

(2) A ♫ note = _____ ♬ notes.

(3) A 𝅗𝅥 note = _____ ♪ notes.

(1) 4

(2) 4

(3) 1

277. Continue as in the preceding frame.

(1) An ♪ note = _____ ♬ notes.

(2) A ♩ note = _____ ♫ notes.

(3) A 𝅗𝅥 note = _____ 𝅗𝅥 notes.

278. RESTS are symbols which represent periods of silence. There is a rest sign which corresponds to each of the basic note values.

| | |
|---|---|
| | double whole rest* |
| | whole rest |
| | half rest |
| | quarter rest |
| | eighth rest |
| | sixteenth rest |
| | thirty-second rest |
| | sixty-fourth rest* |
| | 128th rest* |

Care must be taken not to confuse the whole rest with the half rest. The whole rest hangs from the fourth line of the staff.

Write several whole rests.

*The double whole, sixty-fourth, and 128th rests are rarely used. They will not appear in the remainder of this book.

279. The half rest sits on the third line of the staff. Write several half rests.

280. Write several quarter rests.

281. Write several eighth rests.

282. Write several sixteenth rests.

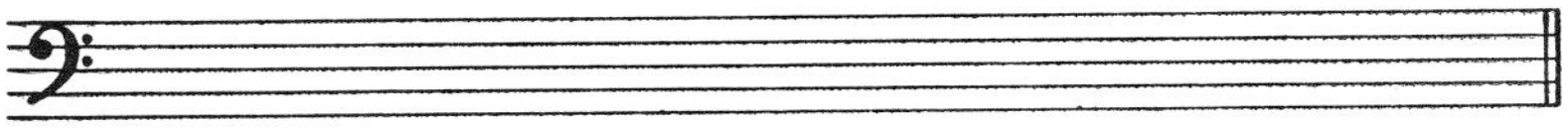

283 Write several thirty-second rests.

(etc.)

(etc.)

(etc.)

(etc.)

(etc.)

**284.** Rests are related to one another in the same way as notes.

A whole rest = 2 half rests.
A whole rest = 4 quarter rests.
A whole rest = 8 eighth rests.

A whole rest equals how many thirty-second rests? _____

32.

---

**285.** Supply the answer in each case.

(1) A ▬ rest = _____ 𝄽 rests.

(2) A ▬ rest = _____ 𝄽 rests.

(3) A ▬ rest = _____ 𝄾 rests.

(1) 4

(2) 2

(3) 4

---

**286.** Supply the answer in each case.

(1) An 𝄾 rest = _____ 𝄿 rests.

(2) A 𝄿 rest = _____ 𝄾 rests.

(3) An 𝄾 rest = _____ 𝄾 rests.

(1) 2

(2) 2

(3) 4

---

**287.** Supply the answer in each case.

(1) A ▬ rest = _____ 𝄾 rests.

(2) A 𝄽 rest = _____ 𝄾 rests.

(3) An 𝄾 rest = _____ 𝄾 rests.

(1) 8

(2) 4

(3) 1

288. A DOT may be added to both notes and rests.*

𝅝· ,   𝅗𝅥· ,   ♩· ,   ♪· , etc.

▬· , ▬· ,   𝄼· ,   𝄽· , etc.

The dot increases the value of a note or rest by one-half of its original value.

𝅗𝅥· = 𝅗𝅥 𝅗𝅥        ▬· = ▬ + 𝄼

♩· = ♩ ♪        𝄼· = 𝄼 + 𝄽

The duration of a dotted note is (longer/shorter) _____ than the same note without the dot.

*Printed music issued by some publishers reveals a tendency not to dot rests, but rather to write separate rests to represent the value desired ( 𝄼 𝄽 instead of 𝄼· , 𝄽 𝄾 instead of 𝄽· , etc.). However, it is correct to dot rests if you wish. Many examples of dotted rests can be found in published music.

longer

289. Complete each problem as in the preceding frame.

(1) 𝅝· = _____ _____ .
                ( ⌣ )

(2) ♪· = _____ _____ .
                ( ⌣ )

(3) ♪· = _____ _____ .
                ( ⌣ )

(1) 𝅝⌢𝅗𝅥

(2) ♪⌢♪

(3) ♪⌢♪

290. Rewrite using dots.

(1) 𝅗𝅥⌢♩ = _____ .

(2) ♪⌢♪ = _____ .

(3) 𝅝⌢𝅗𝅥 = _____ .

(1) 𝅗𝅥·

(2) ♪·

(3) 𝅝·

291. Complete each problem. *(Refer to Frame 288.)*

(1)  + ▬ 

(2) 𝄿 + 𝄾 

(3) 𝄾 + 𝄿 

291. (continued)

(1) ▬̇ = _____ + _____ .

(2) 𝄿˙ = _____ + _____ .

(3) 𝄾˙ = _____ + _____ .

---

292. Rewrite using dots.

(1) 𝄿 

(2) 𝄽˙ 

(3) ▬̇ 

292. (continued)

(1) 𝄿 + 𝄾 = _____ .

(2) 𝄽 + 𝄿 = _____ .

(3) ▬ + 𝄽 = _____ .

---

293. An additional dot may be applied to a dotted note or rest.

𝅗𝅥.. ,    ♩.. ,    ♪.. ,  etc.

▬.. ,    𝄽.. ,    𝄿·· ,  etc.

The second dot increases the value of the note or rest by one-half of the value represented by the first dot.

𝅗𝅥.. =  𝅗𝅥 ⌣ ♩ ⌣ ♪

▬·· = ▬ + 𝄽 + 𝄿

Each successive dot increases the value of the note by (1/8, 1/4, 1/2) _____ the value of the preceding dot.

1/2

**294.** Complete each problem as in the preceding frame.

(1) 𝄽.. = _____ + _____ + _____ .

(2) 𝄾.. = _____ + _____ + _____ .

(3) ▬.. = _____ + _____ + _____ .

(1) 𝄽 + 𝄾 + 𝄿

(2) 𝄾 + 𝄿 + 𝄾

(3) ▬ + 𝄽 + 𝄾

**295.** Complete each problem.

(1) ♩.. = _____ _____ _____
         ( ‿‿‿ ‿‿‿ )

(2) ♪.. = _____ _____ _____
         ( ‿‿‿ ‿‿‿ )

(3) ♩.. = _____ _____ _____
         ( ‿‿‿ ‿‿‿ )

(1) ♩ ♪ ♬

(2) ♪ ♬ ♬

(3) ♩ ♩ ♪

**296.** An undotted note divides naturally into <u>two</u> equal parts.

𝅝 = ♩ ♩
♩ = ♪ ♪
♪ = ♫

Show the natural division of an eighth note.

♪ = _____

297. A dotted note, representing half again as long a duration as the same note without a dot, divides naturally into <u>three</u> equal parts

$$\text{𝅗𝅥.} = \text{𝅘𝅥 𝅘𝅥 𝅘𝅥}$$
$$\text{𝅘𝅥.} = \text{𝅘𝅥𝅮 𝅘𝅥𝅮 𝅘𝅥𝅮}$$
$$\text{𝅘𝅥𝅮.} = \text{𝅘𝅥𝅯 𝅘𝅥𝅯 𝅘𝅥𝅯}$$

Show the natural division of a dotted sixteenth note.

𝅘𝅥𝅯. = _____

---

298. Show (with notes) the division of each note below.

(1) 𝅗𝅥 divides into _____.

(2) 𝅘𝅥 divides into _____.

---

299. Continue as in the preceding frame.

(1) 𝅗𝅥. divides into _____.

(2) 𝅘𝅥. divides into _____.

---

300. Continue as in the preceding frame.

(1) 𝅝 divides into _____.

(2) 𝅘𝅥𝅮. divides into _____.

---

301. Continue as in the preceding frame.

(1) 𝅗𝅥 divides into _____.

(2) 𝅗𝅥. divides into _____.

**(1)** ♫

**(2)** ♪♪♪

302. Continue as in the preceding frame.

(1) ♪ divides into _____ .

(2) ♩. divides into _____ .

---

303. An undotted note subdivides naturally into <u>four</u> equal parts.

𝅗𝅥 subdivides into ♩♩♩♩

♩ subdivides into ♫♫

♪ subdivides into ♬♬

The normal subdivision of an undotted note is into _____ equal parts.

four

---

**(1)** ♫♫

**(2)** ♬♬

304. Show how each note naturally subdivides.

(1) ♩ subdivides into _____ .

(2) ♪ subdivides into _____ .

---

305. A dotted note subdivides naturally into <u>six</u> equal parts.

𝅗𝅥. subdivides into ♩♩♩♩♩♩

♩. subdivides into ♫♫♫

♪. subdivides into ♬♬♬

The natural subdivision of a dotted note is into _____ equal parts.

six

**306.** Show how each note naturally subdivides.

(1) ♪. subdivides into _____ .

(2) ♩. subdivides into _____ .

(1) [music notation: six notes beamed]

(2) [music notation: six notes beamed]

---

**307.** Show how each note naturally subdivides.

(1) ♩ subdivides into _____ .

(2) ♪ subdivides into _____ .

(1) [music notation: four notes beamed]

(2) [music notation: six notes beamed]

---

**308.** By using the proper indication, notes may be subdivided into four, five, six, seven, or more parts.

| FOUR | FIVE | SIX | SEVEN |
|------|------|-----|-------|

Subdivision of an undotted note into five, six, or seven parts, or the subdivision of a dotted note into four, five, or seven parts results in IRREGULAR GROUPS. * Such groups are not the result of a natural division or subdivision and thus may be regarded as "artificial." As shown above, a number is used to indicate how many notes are included in the group.

Is six a natural subdivision of an undotted note?

_____

*The terms "foreign" and "mixed" groups are also used.

No.
*(An undotted note subdivides naturally into four equal parts.)*

*Expository frame.*

309.  There is lack of standardization regarding the note values used to indicate irregular groups. *  A simple and practical principle to follow is to use the note value of the division until the subdivision is reached, and to continue to use the value of the subdivision until the natural division of the subdivision is reached.

(No response required.)

*For further information regarding the notation of irregular divisions see Gardner Read, "Some Problems of Rhythmic Notation," *Journal of Music Theory*, 9/1 (1965), pp. 153-62.

(1)

(2)

310.  Supply the correct notation.

(1)  A ♩ note subdivided into five parts is notated _____ .

(2)  A ♩ note subdivided into seven parts is notated _____ .

---

(1)

(2)

311.  Continue as in the preceding frame.

(1)  An ♪ note subdivided into five parts is notated _____ .

(2)  A ♩. note subdivided into seven parts is notated _____ .

---

(1)

(2)

312.  Continue as in the preceding frame.

(1)  A ♩. note subdivided into four parts is notated _____ .

(2)  A ♩. note subdivided into five parts is notated _____ .

---

Three.

313.  The note which represents the duration of the beat is called the UNIT.

How many units are there in one measure of triple meter? _____

---

Two.

314.  How many units are there in one measure of duple meter? _____

---

Four.

315.  How many units are there in one measure of quadruple meter? _____

| | |
|---|---|
| simple | 316. The UNIT in simple time is always an undotted note, since this type of note divides naturally into <u>two</u> equal parts. Any note may be the UNIT, but the most usual values are the half note, the quarter note, and the eighth note.<br><br>    The unit is always an undotted note in _____ time. |
| three | 317. The UNIT in compound time is always a dotted note, since this type of note divides naturally into <u>three</u> equal parts. The most common units in compound time are the dotted half note, the dotted quarter note, and the dotted eighth note.<br><br>    The dotted note divides naturally into _____ equal parts. |
| unit | 318. The note which represents the duration of the beat is called the _____. |
| two | 319. The undotted note divides naturally into _____ equal parts. |
| compound | 320. The unit is always a dotted note in _____ time. |
| (2) 𝅘𝅥<br>(4) 𝅘𝅥𝅮 | 321. Which of the notes below could represent the beat in <u>simple</u> time? _____<br><br>   (1) 𝅗𝅥.  (2) 𝅘𝅥  (3) 𝅘𝅥𝅮.  (4) 𝅘𝅥𝅮 |

(1) ♩.

(3) ♪.

(4) ♩.

---

**322.** Which of the notes below could be the unit in compound time?_____

(1) ♩. (2) 𝅝 (3) ♪. (4) ♩.

---

Division: ♪ ♪

Subdivision: ♫ ♫

---

**323.** Show the division and subdivision of the unit.

| Unit | Division | Subdivision |
|------|----------|-------------|
| ♩ | _____ | _____ |

---

Division: ♪ ♪

Subdivision: ♫ ♫

---

**324.** Continue as in the preceding frame.

| Unit | Division | Subdivision |
|------|----------|-------------|
| ♪ | _____ | _____ |

---

Division: ♩ ♩ ♩

Subdivision: ♫ ♫ ♫

---

**325.** Continue as in the preceding frame.

| Unit | Division | Subdivision |
|------|----------|-------------|
| ♩. | _____ | _____ |

Division: ♩ ♪ ♪ ♪

Subdivision: ♫♫♫♫♫♫

**326.** Continue as in the preceding frame.

| Unit | Division | Subdivision |
|------|----------|-------------|
| ♩. | _____ | _____ |

Division: ♪ ♫

Subdivision: ♫♫♫♫

**327.** Continue as in the preceding frame.

| Unit | Division | Subdivision |
|------|----------|-------------|
| ♪ | _____ | _____ |

Division: ♩ ♩

Subdivision: ♩♩♩♩

**328.** Continue as in the preceding frame.

| Unit | Division | Subdivision |
|------|----------|-------------|
| 𝅗𝅥 | _____ | _____ |

𝅗𝅥

♩

♪

**329.** Indicate the most common units in <u>simple</u> time: (1) _____; (2) _____; (3) _____.

𝅗𝅥.

♩.

♪.

**330.** Indicate the most common units in <u>compound</u> time: (1) _____; (2) _____; (3) _____.

331. Notes, in themselves, represent only relative duration. Exact duration can be indicated by establishing the rate of the unit. A sign at the beginning of a composition such as M.M. ♩=60* (or simply ♩ = 60), indicates that the quarter note is to progress at the rate of 60 per minute.

    With the same indication (♩ = 60), what is the rate of the eighth note? _____ per minute.

120

*The two M's stand for Mälzel Metronome. In 1816 Mälzel invented an instrument based upon the principle of the double pendulum which could be set to indicate a given number of beats per minute. Beethoven was one of the first composers to make use of metronome indications in his music.

144

332. If the indication is ♩ = 72, what is the rate of the quarter note? _____ per minute.

180

333. If the indication is ♩. = 60, what is the rate of the eighth note? _____ per minute.

60

334. If the indication is ♩ = 120, what is the rate of the whole note? _____ per minute.

48

335. If the indication is ♪. = 96, what is the rate of the dotted quarter note? _____ per minute.

*Expository frame.*

336. Composers often use Italian (sometimes English, German, or French) terms to indicate the approximate speed and character of their music. Some of the most common terms are listed below:*

| | |
|---|---|
| *Prestissimo* | Extremely fast |
| *Presto* | Very fast |
| *Allegro* | Fast |
| *Allegretto* | Fast, but slower than *allegro* |
| *Moderato* | Moderate |
| *Andante* | Moderately slow |
| *Adagio* | Slow |
| *Largo* | Extremely slow |

Terms such as these do not indicate the precise speed of a composition; this can be done only by making use of the metronome.

*Consult the Glossary of Musical Terms, p. 245, for other tempo and phrasing indications commonly found in music.

*(No response required.)*

337. The basic rhythmic organization of SIMPLE TIME is shown below:

The note which represents the duration of the beat is called the UNIT. The quarter note is often used as the unit, but we should not think of the quarter note as always "getting the beat." The eighth note and the half note are also used as units in _____ time.

simple

338. The basic rhythmic organization of COMPOUND TIME is shown below:

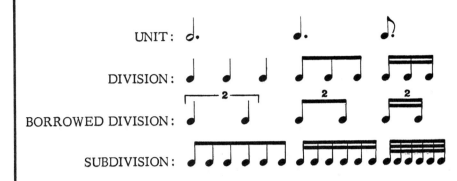

The unit in compound time is always a(n) (dotted/ undotted) _____ note.

dotted

## SUMMARY

The rhythmic element of music elicits from the listener a very elemental response. Rapid beats and animated rhythmic patterns excite; slow beats and relatively simple patterns have the opposite effect. Precise notation for the duration of tones and silences is vital to accurate performance.

There are two basic types of notes: (1) undotted notes divide naturally into two equal parts and represent the beat in simple time; (2) dotted notes divide naturally into three equal parts and represent the beat in compound time. The division of the beat into three equal parts in simple time, and two equal parts in compound time results in borrowed divisions. The normal subdivision of the beat in simple time is into four equal parts; in compound time it is into six equal parts. Subdivisions of five and seven in simple time, and four, five, seven, eight, nine, ten, and eleven in compound time are called irregular groups.

# 5
# Time Signatures

The beat is the simplest manifestation of rhythm. It is given added musical significance by various patterns of stress called meters. Additional rhythmic interest results from the division of the beat into either two equal parts (simple time), or three equal parts (compound time). Time signatures indicate not only the meter, but also whether the division of the beat is simple or compound.

---

compound

---

(1) $\frac{6}{2}$

(4) $\frac{9}{4}$

---

339. The metrical organization of a musical composition is indicated by a TIME SIGNATURE. * A time signature consists of two numbers placed on the staff one above the other at the beginning of the composition. There are two types of time signatures: those which indicate simple time, and those which indicate compound time.

   This is how you can distinguish between simple and compound time signatures: *If the upper number is 6, 9, 12, or 15, the time signature represents COMPOUND time. Any number other than these means that the signature represents SIMPLE time.*

   If the upper number of the time signature is 6, 9, 12, or 15, the signature represents _____ time.

*Time signatures are also called meter signatures.

---

340. Which of the following time signatures indicate compound time? _____

   (1) $\frac{6}{2}$   (2) $\frac{5}{4}$   (3) $\frac{3}{8}$   (4) $\frac{9}{4}$

(2) $\frac{2}{4}$

(3) $\frac{4}{8}$

341. Which of the following time signatures indicate simple time? _____

(1) $\frac{12}{8}$   (2) $\frac{2}{4}$   (3) $\frac{4}{8}$   (4) $\frac{6}{4}$

---

6, 9, 12, 15.

342. What numbers are found in the upper part of compound time signatures?

_____

---

1, 2, 3, 4, 5, 7, 8.
*(Others are possible,
but not practical.)*

343. Write some of the numbers which could be found in the upper part of simple time signatures.

_____

---

upper number

344. The upper number of the time signature tells us the number of beats per measure. Whether the meter is DUPLE, TRIPLE, QUADRUPLE, or QUINTUPLE is shown by the _____ _____ of the time signature.

---

(1) 3

(2) 4

(3) 5

345. The upper number of simple time signatures directly indicates the number of beats per measure.

$\frac{2}{4}$ = 2 beats per measure

Show the number of beats per measure indicated by each of the simple time signatures below:

(1) $\frac{3}{2}$ = _____ beats per measure.

(2) $\frac{4}{4}$ = _____ beats per measure.

(3) $\frac{5}{4}$ = _____ beats per measure.

346. The upper number of <u>compound</u> time signatures does not directly indicate the number of beats per measure as was the case in simple time. In order to determine the number of beats per measure, the upper number of compound time signatures must be divided by three.

$$\frac{6}{4} \div 3 = 2 \text{ beats per measure.}$$

Show the number of beats per measure indicated by each of the compound time signatures below:

(1) $\frac{9}{8}$ = _____ beats per measure.

(2) $\frac{12}{8}$ = _____ beats per measure.

(3) $\frac{15}{8}$ = _____ beats per measure.

(1) 3

(2) 4

(3) 5

---

347. The upper number of the time signature directly indicates the number of beats per measure in _____ time.

simple

---

348. In order to determine the number of beats per measure in compound time the upper number of the time signature must be divided by _____.

three

---

349. Show the number of beats per measure indicated by each of the time signatures below (<u>determine first whether each is a simple or compound signature</u>):

(1) $\frac{2}{8}$ = _____ beats per measure.

(2) $\frac{6}{4}$ = _____ beats per measure.

(3) $\frac{4}{2}$ = _____ beats per measure.

(1) 2

(2) 2

(3) 4

(1) 5

(2) 3

(3) 4

350. Continue as in the preceding frame.

    (1) $\frac{5}{8}$ = _____ beats per measure.

    (2) $\frac{9}{4}$ = _____ beats per measure.

    (3) $\frac{12}{16}$ = _____ beats per measure.

---

(1) 3

(2) 7

(3) 5

351. Continue as in the preceding frame.

    (1) $\frac{3}{2}$ = _____ beats per measure.

    (2) $\frac{7}{8}$ = _____ beats per measure.

    (3) $\frac{15}{8}$ = _____ beats per measure.

---

Each pair indicates the same number of beats per measure:
(1) two beats,
(2) three beats,
(3) four beats.

352. What does each pair of time signatures below have in common?

    (1) $\frac{2}{4} - \frac{6}{8}$    (2) $\frac{3}{8} - \frac{9}{4}$    (3) $\frac{4}{4} - \frac{12}{8}$

_____

_____

---

lower

353. From the upper number of the time signature we deduce the meter (the number of beats per measure). The UNIT is indicated by the lower number, but simple and compound signatures must be interpreted differently.

    The kind of note which represents the beat is deduced from the (upper/lower) _____ number of the time signature.

354. The lower number of <u>simple</u> time signatures directly indicates the UNIT.

$$\frac{2}{4} \quad \text{Unit:} \quad \text{\musQuarter}$$

(The number 4 represents a quarter note.)

Show the unit indicated by each of the simple time signatures below:

(1) $\frac{5}{2}$ Unit = _____ .

(2) $\frac{3}{8}$ Unit = _____ .

(3) $\frac{4}{4}$ Unit = _____ .

---

(1) \musHalf

(2) \musEighth

(3) \musQuarter

355. The lower number in <u>compound</u> time signatures represents the DIVISION of the UNIT.

$$\frac{6}{8} \quad \text{Division} = \quad \text{\musEighth}$$

(The number 8 represents an eighth note.)

Show the division indicated by each of the compound time signatures below:

(1) $\frac{12}{16}$ Division = _____

(2) $\frac{6}{8}$ Division = _____

(3) $\frac{9}{4}$ Division = _____

---

(1) \musEighth

(2) \musEighth

(3) \musQuarter

356. The lower number of <u>simple</u> time signatures indicates the unit.

The lower number of <u>compound</u> time signatures indicates the _____ .

---

division

357. The UNIT in compound time consists of three divisions. Thus, three divisions combine to make the UNIT.

$$\frac{6}{8} \text{ Division } = \eighthnote$$

$$\eighthnote\eighthnote\eighthnote = \dottedquarternote \quad \text{(The UNIT)}$$

In compound time a note which is equal in value to three divisions is called the _____ .

unit

---

358. The unit in compound time is equal in value to three _____ .

divisions

---

359. The unit in compound time is always a DOTTED note.*

Show the unit indicated by each of the compound time signatures below:

(1) $\frac{9}{8}$ Unit = _____

(2) $\frac{6}{4}$ Unit = _____

(3) $\frac{12}{8}$ Unit = _____

*In a very slow tempo it may be more convenient to assign the beat to the division rather than the unit. Duple-compound meter, for example, might be counted as a six-beat measure. However, chord changes, rhythmic patterns, phrase structure, and the location of cadences will usually give evidence to the underlying duple organization.

(1)  dotted quarter note

(2) dotted half note

(3) dotted quarter note

(1) ♩.

(2) ♪.

(3) ♩.

dotted

undotted

(1) ♩.

(2) ♩

(3) ♩.

360. Continue as in the preceding frame.

    (1) $\frac{15}{8}$ Unit = _____

    (2) $\frac{6}{16}$ Unit = _____

    (3) $\frac{9}{4}$ Unit = _____

361. In compound time the lower number of the time signature indicates the division. Three divisions combine to make the unit. The unit in compound time is always a(n) (dotted/undotted) _____ note.

362. In simple time the lower number of the time signature directly indicates the unit. The unit in simple time is always a(n) (dotted/undotted) _____ note.

363. Show the unit indicated by each of the time signatures below (<u>determine first whether each is a simple or compound signature</u>):

    (1) $\frac{9}{8}$ Unit = _____

    (2) $\frac{2}{4}$ Unit = _____

    (3) $\frac{12}{4}$ Unit = _____

(1)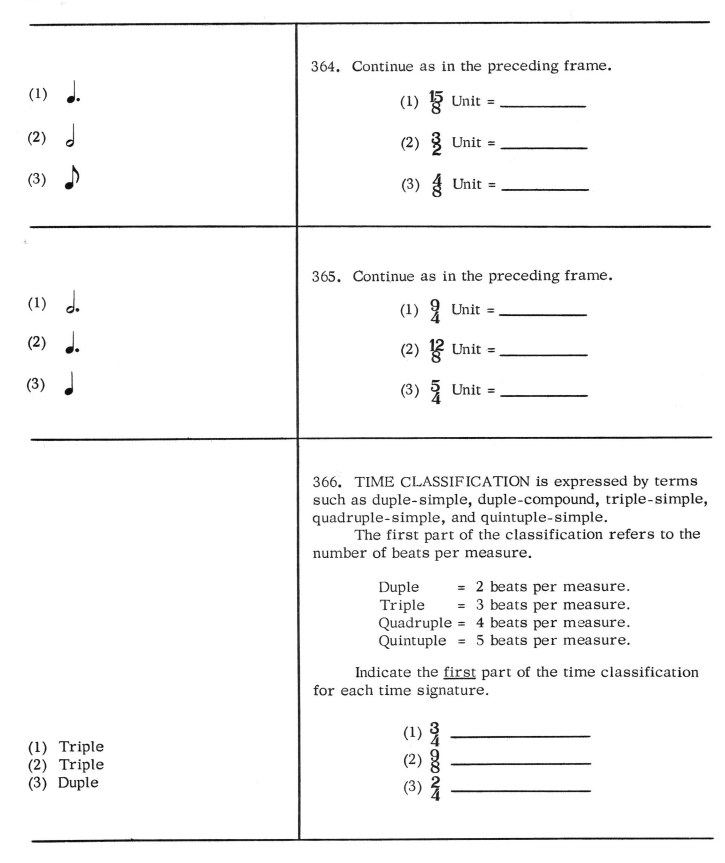

(2)

(3)

364. Continue as in the preceding frame.

    (1) $\frac{15}{8}$ Unit = _____

    (2) $\frac{3}{2}$ Unit = _____

    (3) $\frac{4}{8}$ Unit = _____

---

(1)

(2)

(3)

365. Continue as in the preceding frame.

    (1) $\frac{9}{4}$ Unit = _____

    (2) $\frac{12}{8}$ Unit = _____

    (3) $\frac{5}{4}$ Unit = _____

---

366. TIME CLASSIFICATION is expressed by terms such as duple-simple, duple-compound, triple-simple, quadruple-simple, and quintuple-simple.

The first part of the classification refers to the number of beats per measure.

    Duple     = 2 beats per measure.
    Triple    = 3 beats per measure.
    Quadruple = 4 beats per measure.
    Quintuple = 5 beats per measure.

Indicate the <u>first</u> part of the time classification for each time signature.

    (1) $\frac{3}{4}$ _____

    (2) $\frac{9}{8}$ _____

    (3) $\frac{2}{4}$ _____

(1) Triple
(2) Triple
(3) Duple

| | |
|---|---|
| (1) Duple<br><br>(2) Quadruple<br><br>(3) Quadruple | 367. Continue as in the preceding frame.<br><br>(1) $\frac{6}{8}$ _____<br>(2) $\frac{4}{4}$ _____<br>(3) $\frac{12}{8}$ _____ |
| (1) Quintuple<br><br>(2) Triple<br><br>(3) Quintuple | 368. Continue as in the preceding frame.<br><br>(1) $\frac{5}{4}$ _____<br>(2) $\frac{3}{2}$ _____<br>(3) $\frac{15}{8}$ _____ |
| (1) Triple<br><br>(2) Duple<br><br>(3) Quadruple | 369. Continue as in the preceding frame.<br><br>(1) $\frac{3}{8}$ _____<br>(2) $\frac{6}{4}$ _____<br>(3) $\frac{4}{8}$ _____ |
| (1) Simple<br><br>(2) Simple<br><br>(3) Compound | 370. The second part of the time classification tells whether the beat is divided into <u>two</u> parts (simple time), or <u>three</u> parts (compound time). It also tells whether the unit is an undotted or a dotted note.<br><br>    Indicate the <u>second</u> part of the time classification for each time signature.<br><br>(1) $\frac{2}{4}$ _____<br>(2) $\frac{3}{8}$ _____<br>(3) $\frac{9}{8}$ _____ |

371. Continue as in the preceding frame.

(1) Compound

(1) $\dfrac{12}{4}$ _____

(2) Simple

(2) $\dfrac{5}{8}$ _____

(3) Compound

(3) $\dfrac{6}{4}$ _____

372. Continue as in the preceding frame.

(1) Compound

(1) $\dfrac{15}{8}$ _____

(2) Simple

(2) $\dfrac{3}{4}$ _____

(3) Simple

(3) $\dfrac{7}{8}$ _____

373. The time classification of simple time signatures is interpreted as below:

Time signature:
$\begin{cases} \dfrac{3}{4} = 3 \text{ beats per measure - TRIPLE} \\ \dfrac{3}{4} = \text{Unit: } \; ; \text{ Div.: } \; \text{ - SIMPLE} \end{cases}$

Time Classification:  TRIPLE-SIMPLE

Supply the time classification for each of the time signatures below:

(1) Quadruple-simple

(1) $\dfrac{4}{4}$ _____ - _____

(2) Quintuple-simple

(2) $\dfrac{5}{8}$ _____ - _____

(3) Duple-simple

(3) $\dfrac{2}{2}$ _____ - _____

**374.** The time classification of compound time signatures is interpreted as below:

Time signature: $\begin{cases} \dfrac{9}{8} \div 3 = 3 \text{ beats per measure - TRIPLE} \\ \dfrac{9}{8} = \text{Div.:} \ \eighthnote; \ \text{♫♫} = \dotted{quarternote} \ \text{(Unit) - COMPOUND} \end{cases}$

Time Classification:  TRIPLE-COMPOUND

Supply the time classification for each of the time signatures below:

(1) $\dfrac{6}{2}$ _____ - _____

(2) $\dfrac{12}{16}$ _____ - _____

(3) $\dfrac{15}{16}$ _____ - _____

1) Duple-compound

(2) Quadruple-compound

(3) Quintuple-compound

---

**375.** Continue as in the preceding frame.

(1) $\dfrac{4}{8}$ _____ - _____

(2) $\dfrac{6}{16}$ _____ - _____

(3) $\dfrac{3}{2}$ _____ - _____

(1) Quadruple-simple

(2) Duple-compound

(3) Triple-simple

---

**376.** Continue as in the preceding frame.

(1) $\dfrac{9}{4}$ _____ - _____

(2) $\dfrac{4}{2}$ _____ - _____

(3) $\dfrac{12}{8}$ _____ - _____

(1) Triple-compound

(2) Quadruple-simple

(3) Quadruple-compound

No.

*(It must be divided by three.)*

---

377. In simple time the upper number directly indicates the number of beats per measure.

    Does the upper number in compound time signatures directly indicate the number of beats per measure? _____

---

6.

---

378. Notice the relation of the upper number of the time signature to the number of beats per measure in compound time:

| Upper Number | Beats per Measure | Meter |
|:---:|:---:|:---|
| 6 | 2 | Duple |
| 9 | 3 | Triple |
| 12 | 4 | Quadruple |
| 15 | 5 | Quintuple |

    In simple time DUPLE meter is indicated by the number 2. What is the upper number of the time signature in DUPLE-COMPOUND time? _____

---

$\frac{3}{2}$   $\frac{3}{4}$   $\frac{3}{8}$   $\frac{3}{16}$

*(Any three.)*

---

379. Supply three of the possible time signatures for the time classification below:

    Triple-simple _____ _____ _____

---

$\frac{6}{4}$   $\frac{6}{8}$   $\frac{6}{16}$

---

380. Continue as in the preceding frame.

    Duple-compound _____ _____ _____

| | |
|---|---|
| $\frac{9}{4}$ $\frac{9}{8}$ $\frac{9}{16}$ | 381. Continue as in the preceding frame.<br><br>Triple-compound \_\_\_\_\_ \_\_\_\_\_ \_\_\_\_\_ |
| $\frac{2}{2}$ $\frac{2}{4}$ $\frac{2}{8}$ $\frac{2}{16}$<br>*(Any three.)* | 382. Continue as in the preceding frame.<br><br>Duple-simple \_\_\_\_\_ \_\_\_\_\_ \_\_\_\_\_ |
| $\frac{4}{2}$ $\frac{4}{4}$ $\frac{4}{8}$ $\frac{4}{16}$<br>*(Any three.)* | 383. Continue as in the preceding frame.<br><br>Quadruple-simple \_\_\_\_\_ \_\_\_\_\_ \_\_\_\_\_ |
| $\frac{15}{4}$ $\frac{15}{8}$ $\frac{15}{16}$ | 384. Continue as in the preceding frame.<br><br>Quintuple-compound \_\_\_\_\_ \_\_\_\_\_ \_\_\_\_\_ |
| $\frac{12}{4}$ $\frac{12}{8}$ $\frac{12}{16}$ | 385. Continue as in the preceding frame.<br><br>Quadruple-compound \_\_\_\_\_ \_\_\_\_\_ \_\_\_\_\_ |
| $\frac{5}{2}$ $\frac{5}{4}$ $\frac{5}{8}$ $\frac{5}{16}$<br>*(Any three.)* | 386. Continue as in the preceding frame.<br><br>Quintuple-simple \_\_\_\_\_ \_\_\_\_\_ \_\_\_\_\_ |

**C**

387. Two time signatures (**C** and **₵** ) are vestiges of earlier systems of notation.  The sign (**C**) stands for the signature $\frac{4}{4}$ (quadruple-simple) and is called COMMON TIME.

Common time is the same as quadruple-simple. Write the signature for common time. _____

---

duple-
simple

388. The signature (**₵**) is called ALLA BREVE.  This indicates a quick duple-simple meter, in which the half note receives the beat.  It is the equivalent of $\frac{2}{2}$ time.

The time classification of <u>alla breve</u> is _____-
_____ .

---

**₵**

389. Write the signature for <u>alla breve</u>. _____

| | |
|---|---|
| Four. | 390. How many beats per measure are indicated by the signature **C**?_____ |
| Two. | 391. How many beats per measure are indicated by the signature **₵** ? _____ |
| ♩ | 392. Write the unit in <u>common time</u>. _____ |
| 𝅗𝅥 | 393. Write the unit in <u>alla breve</u>. _____ |
| tie | 394. The TIE is a curved line which connects two notes of the same pitch in order to express a longer duration.<br><br>The duration of one note value can be added to the duration of another by the use of a _____. |

### 395. TIES BETWEEN UNITS IN SIMPLE TIME

Some typical patterns:

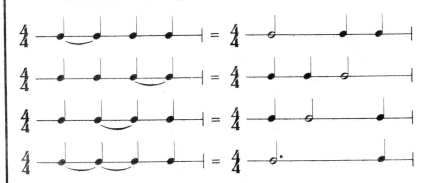

Rewrite without ties (as above) the following rhythm:

### 396. TIES BETWEEN UNITS IN COMPOUND TIME

Some typical patterns:

Rewrite without ties (as above) the following rhythm:

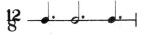

### 397.  TIES BETWEEN DIVISIONS IN SIMPLE TIME

Some typical patterns:

Borrowed division:

Rewrite without ties (as above) the following rhythm:

### 398.  Rewrite without ties the following rhythm;

### 399.  Continue as in the preceding frame.

### 400.  Continue as in the preceding frame.

**401.** TIES BETWEEN DIVISIONS IN COMPOUND TIME

Some typical patterns:

Rewrite the rhythm below without ties:

**402.** Rewrite the rhythm below without ties:

**403.** Continue as in the preceding frame.

**404.** Continue as in the preceding frame.

405. TYPICAL SUBDIVISION PATTERNS IN SIMPLE
TIME
Unit: ♩

Rewrite the rhythm below without ties:

406. Rewrite the rhythm below without ties:

407. Continue as in the preceding frame.

408.

408. Continue as in the preceding frame.

409. TYPICAL SUBDIVISION PATTERNS IN
     COMPOUND TIME*
     Unit: ♩.

Rewrite the rhythm below without ties:

*Subdivision patterns in compound time are so numerous
that only the most common are shown.

410. Rewrite the rhythm below without ties:

411. Continue as in the preceding frame.

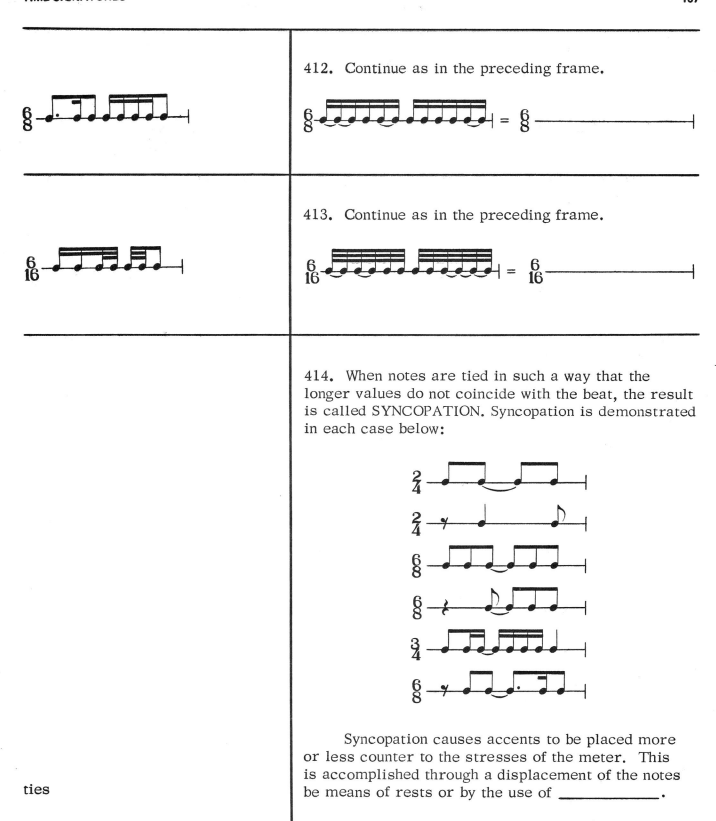

412. Continue as in the preceding frame.

413. Continue as in the preceding frame.

414. When notes are tied in such a way that the longer values do not coincide with the beat, the result is called SYNCOPATION. Syncopation is demonstrated in each case below:

Syncopation causes accents to be placed more or less counter to the stresses of the meter. This is accomplished through a displacement of the notes be means of rests or by the use of _____.

ties

415. Notes which occur within a beat are usually beamed together.

Notice that in each example the total value of the notes in every beat is the same. The sum of the note values must equal the value of the UNIT in all cases.

Group the notes by using beams instead of flags so that the meter is clearly expressed.

416. Group the notes by using beams instead of flags so that the meter is clearly expressed.

417. Continue as in the preceding frame.

$\frac{6}{8}$

**418.** Continue as in the preceding frame.

$\frac{6}{8}$ = $\frac{6}{8}$

$\frac{3}{4}$

**419.** Continue as in the preceding frame.

$\frac{3}{4}$ = $\frac{3}{4}$

$\frac{6}{4}$

**420.** Continue as in the preceding frame.

$\frac{6}{4}$ = $\frac{6}{4}$

$\frac{9}{8}$

**421.** Continue as in the preceding frame.

$\frac{9}{8}$ = $\frac{9}{8}$

**422.** Each of the examples below is a complete measure. Select the correct time signature from the alternatives supplied.

(1) $\frac{3}{8}$

(2) $\frac{6}{4}$

(3) **C**

(1) $\frac{6}{8}$  $\frac{2}{4}$  $\frac{3}{8}$  $\frac{5}{16}$ ____

(2) $\frac{3}{2}$  $\frac{12}{8}$  $\frac{5}{2}$  $\frac{6}{4}$ ____

(3) $\frac{7}{8}$  **C**  $\frac{6}{4}$  $\frac{2}{1}$ ____

(1) $\dfrac{5}{8}$

(2) $\dfrac{6}{8}$

(3) $\dfrac{2}{4}$

**423.** Continue as in the preceding frame.

(1) $\dfrac{2}{4}$ $\dfrac{3}{4}$ $\dfrac{5}{8}$ $\dfrac{2}{2}$ ___

(2) $\dfrac{6}{8}$ $\dfrac{3}{4}$ $\dfrac{7}{8}$ $\dfrac{2}{2}$ ___

(3) $\mathbf{C}$ $\dfrac{2}{4}$ $\dfrac{5}{8}$ $\dfrac{3}{8}$ ___

---

(1) $\dfrac{12}{8}$

(2) $\dfrac{4}{4}$

(3) $\dfrac{3}{8}$

**424.** Continue as in the preceding frame.

(1) $\dfrac{4}{4}$ $\dfrac{2}{2}$ $\dfrac{6}{4}$ $\dfrac{12}{8}$ ___

(2) $\dfrac{4}{4}$ $\dfrac{3}{2}$ $\dfrac{7}{8}$ $\dfrac{5}{4}$ ___

(3) $\mathbf{C}$ $\dfrac{6}{8}$ $\dfrac{3}{8}$ $\dfrac{9}{16}$ ___

---

(1) $\dfrac{2}{2}$

(2) $\dfrac{9}{4}$

(3) $\dfrac{3}{4}$

**425.** Continue as in the preceding frame.

(1) $\dfrac{5}{4}$ $\dfrac{2}{2}$ $\dfrac{3}{4}$ $\dfrac{6}{4}$ ___

(2) $\dfrac{3}{2}$ $\dfrac{9}{4}$ $\dfrac{5}{2}$ $\dfrac{3}{1}$ ___

(3) $\dfrac{3}{4}$ $\dfrac{7}{8}$ $\dfrac{4}{4}$ $\dfrac{5}{8}$ ___

(1)  $\frac{5}{4}$

(2)  $\frac{3}{2}$

(3)  $\frac{6}{16}$

426.  Continue as in the preceding frame.

(1)  $\frac{4}{4}$  $\frac{9}{8}$  $\frac{5}{4}$  $\frac{12}{8}$  ___

(2)  $\frac{6}{4}$  $\frac{5}{4}$  C  $\frac{3}{2}$  ___

(3)  $\frac{3}{8}$  $\frac{6}{16}$  $\frac{2}{4}$  $\frac{4}{16}$  ___

## SUMMARY

Time signatures are interpreted differently depending on whether they represent simple or compound time.  The upper number of simple time signatures indicates the number of beats per measure (meter), and the lower number represents the unit.  In the case of compound time signatures, however, the upper number must be divided by three to ascertain the number of beats per measure, and since the lower number represents the division rather than the unit, three of the notes represented by this number must be combined to produce the unit.  Notes which occur in a single beat, or some other metric unit such as the measure, are usually beamed together whenever possible.  This is to facilitate the interpretation of rhythmic patterns by making a graphic representation of the pulse.

# 6
# Intervals

Two tones sounding either simultaneously or successively produce an interval. Because intervals are basic building blocks for both melody and harmony, knowledge about them is essential for more advanced work in music theory as well as for the development of fluent reading and performance. In this chapter you will learn to write intervals and also to apply the terminology used to classify them.

| | |
|---|---|
| melodic | 427. Two tones sounding simultaneously produce a HARMONIC interval. A MELODIC interval occurs when two tones are sounded successively.<br><br>The interval below is a (harmonic/melodic) _____ interval. |
| harmonic | 428. The interval below is a (harmonic/melodic) _____ interval. |
| difference | 429. Our concern now is to learn the terminology used to classify the difference in pitch between the two tones of an interval. When the difference in pitch is relatively great, the tones sound "far apart," and the interval seems "large." When the difference is relatively little, the tones sound "close together," and the interval seems "small."<br><br>Intervals vary in size depending on the _____ in pitch between the two tones which constitute them. |

430. There are various methods of classifying intervals. In the field of acoustics (the scientific study of sound), for example, intervals are classified mathematically as the ratio between the frequencies of the two tones. But this is a specialized approach seldom used in practical musical terminology. In music theory, intervals are classified numerically from 1 to 8, according to the number of basic notes encompassed by the interval.

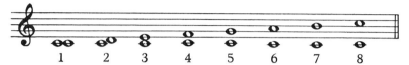

The basic classification of intervals is numerical. The numbers _____ to _____ are used to make this classification.

1 (to) 8

---

431. The numerical classification of intervals is very easy to determine. Merely count the number of basic notes encompassed by the interval. Remember: *both the lower and upper notes are part of the interval.* Call the lower note 1, and count lines and spaces to include the upper note.

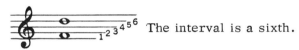 The interval is a sixth.

Indicate the numerical classification of each interval.

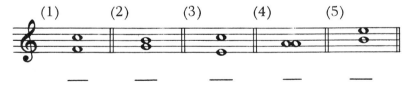

_____ _____ _____ _____ _____

---

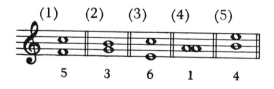

5  3  6  1  4

---

432. Indicate the numerical classification of each interval.

_____ _____ _____ _____ _____

---

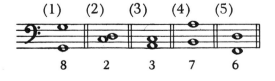

8  2  3  7  6

433. The intervals which have been designated 1 and 8 have special names derived from Latin numeration: 1 = unison,* 8 = octave. It is customary to use ordinal numbers when referring to the remaining intervals.

     1   unison   (or prime)
     2   second   (2nd)
     3   third    (3rd)
     4   fourth   (4th)
     5   fifth    (5th)
     6   sixth    (6th)
     7   seventh  (7th)
     8   octave   (8ve)

An interval which encompasses eight lines and spaces is called a(n) _____.

*The term <u>prime</u> is also used.

octave

---

434. Intervals larger than an octave are called COMPOUND INTERVALS.

    9th      10th     11th     12th

All compound intervals are larger than an _____.

octave

---

435. Occasionally it is necessary to refer to compound intervals as 9ths, 10ths, 11ths, etc., but often they are analyzed as simple intervals (within a single octave). The relation of certain compound intervals to simple intervals is shown below:

Compound:  9th     10th    11th    12th
  Simple:  2nd     3rd     4th     5th

If reduced in size by the interval of an octave, a 12th becomes a _____.

5th

3rd

436. The example below shows that the interval of a 10th consists of an octave plus a _____.

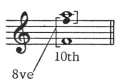

Note: Compound intervals are classed the same as their smaller counterparts; so they need be of no further concern in this study.

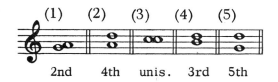

2nd    4th    unis.    3rd    5th

437. Write intervals <u>above</u> the notes as directed.

2nd       4th       unis.       3rd       5th

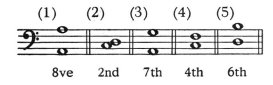

8ve    2nd    7th    4th    6th

438. Write intervals <u>above</u> the notes as directed.

8ve       2nd       7th       4th       6th

439. Intervals may be written below a note by counting <u>down</u> the required number of lines and spaces. To write a 7th below C, for example, call the third space 1, and count down seven lines and spaces.

7th

F.

What note is a 5th below C? _____

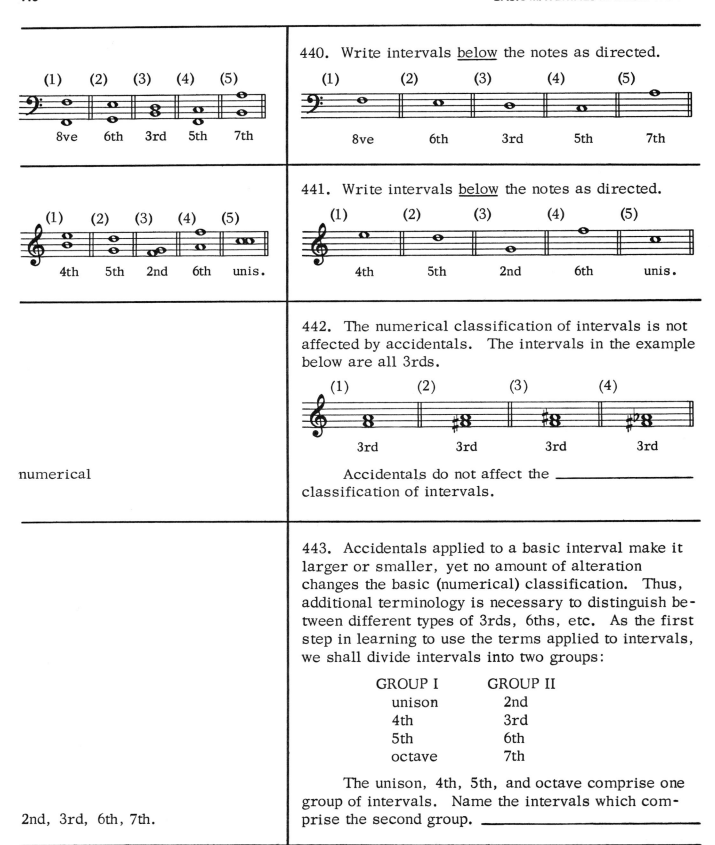

**440.** Write intervals <u>below</u> the notes as directed.

    (1)      (2)      (3)      (4)      (5)

  8ve      6th     3rd     5th     7th

**441.** Write intervals <u>below</u> the notes as directed.

    (1)      (2)      (3)      (4)      (5)

  4th     5th    2nd    6th    unis.

**442.** The numerical classification of intervals is not affected by accidentals. The intervals in the example below are all 3rds.

    (1)        (2)        (3)        (4)

   3rd      3rd      3rd      3rd

numerical

    Accidentals do not affect the _____ classification of intervals.

**443.** Accidentals applied to a basic interval make it larger or smaller, yet no amount of alteration changes the basic (numerical) classification. Thus, additional terminology is necessary to distinguish between different types of 3rds, 6ths, etc. As the first step in learning to use the terms applied to intervals, we shall divide intervals into two groups:

| GROUP I | GROUP II |
|---------|----------|
| unison | 2nd |
| 4th | 3rd |
| 5th | 6th |
| octave | 7th |

2nd, 3rd, 6th, 7th.

    The unison, 4th, 5th, and octave comprise one group of intervals. Name the intervals which comprise the second group. _____

| | |
|---|---|
| Unison, 4th, 5th, 8ve. | 444. Name the intervals of Group I. _____ <br> _____ |
| d. | 445. The intervals of Group I (unison, 4th, 5th, and 8ve) use the terms PERFECT, AUGMENTED, and DIMINISHED. * These terms are abbreviated as below: <br><br>     Perfect      P <br>     Augmented   A <br>     Diminished   d <br><br>     A capital P is used to symbolize the term perfect; a capital A is used to symbolize the term augmented. What is the symbol for the term diminished? _____ <br><br> *There is one exception: the unison cannot be diminished (see Frame 451). |
| No. | 446. A PERFECT UNISON consists of two tones of the same pitch and notation. <br><br>     Is there any difference in pitch between the two tones which produce a perfect unison? _____ |
| (1)     (2)     (3) <br> | 447. Write the note which will produce a perfect unison in each case. <br><br> Write here <br> |

---

**448.** The unison is <u>augmented</u> if one tone is a half-step higher or lower than the other.

The two notes which comprise the augmented unison must have the same letter name. (True/False)
_____

True.

---

**449.** Write the note which will produce an augmented unison <u>above</u> the given note in each case. (Remember: *the augmented unison is a chromatic alteration of the same basic note*.)

---

**450.** Write the note which will produce an augmented unison <u>below</u> the given note in each case.

---

**451.** The term augmented is used for an interval which is one half-step <u>larger</u> than a perfect interval. In the case of a perfect unison, there is no difference in pitch between the two tones, whereas the difference is one half-step in the case of an augmented unison.

    The term diminished is used for an interval which is one half-step <u>smaller</u> than a perfect interval. Since the frequency of two tones cannot be less than zero (perfect unison), the diminished unison is impossible. The other intervals of Group I, however, may be diminished as well as perfect or augmented.

    Unisons may be either _____ or _____, but not diminished.

perfect (or) augmented
*(Any order.)*

**452.** A perfect octave is the same as a perfect unison except that one note is displaced by the interval of an octave.

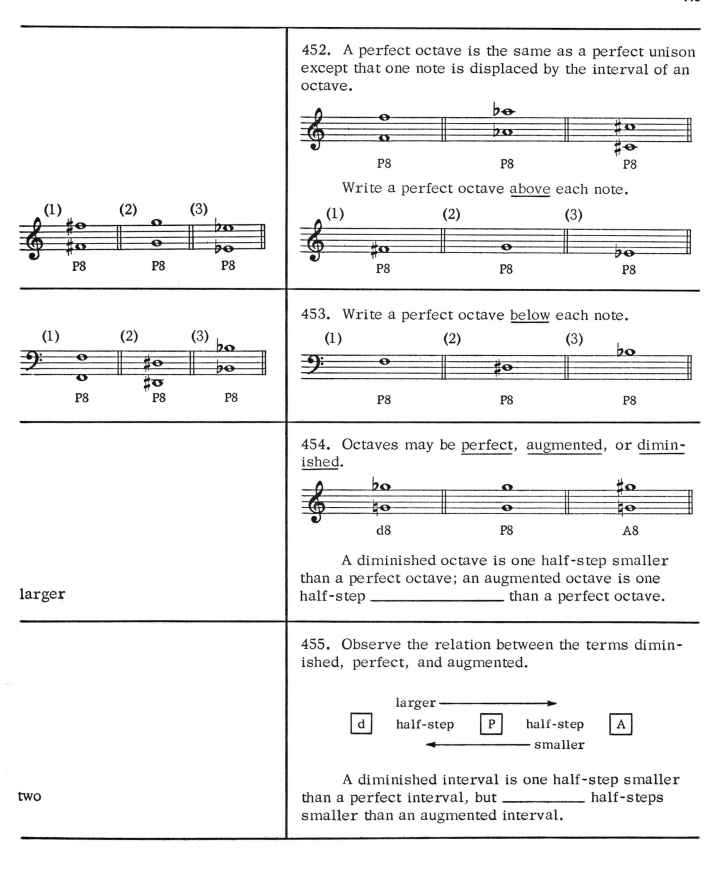

P8          P8          P8

Write a perfect octave <u>above</u> each note.

(1)                    (2)                    (3)

P8                     P8                     P8

(1)          (2)          (3)

P8          P8          P8

**453.** Write a perfect octave <u>below</u> each note.

(1)                    (2)                    (3)

P8                     P8                     P8

(1)          (2)          (3)

P8          P8          P8

**454.** Octaves may be <u>perfect</u>, <u>augmented</u>, or <u>diminished</u>.

d8                     P8                     A8

A diminished octave is one half-step smaller than a perfect octave; an augmented octave is one half-step _____ than a perfect octave.

larger

**455.** Observe the relation between the terms diminished, perfect, and augmented.

larger ————————————→

| d |   half-step   | P |   half-step   | A |

←———————— smaller

A diminished interval is one half-step smaller than a perfect interval, but _____ half-steps smaller than an augmented interval.

two

**456.** A perfect octave is made augmented by <u>increasing</u> the difference in pitch by one half-step.

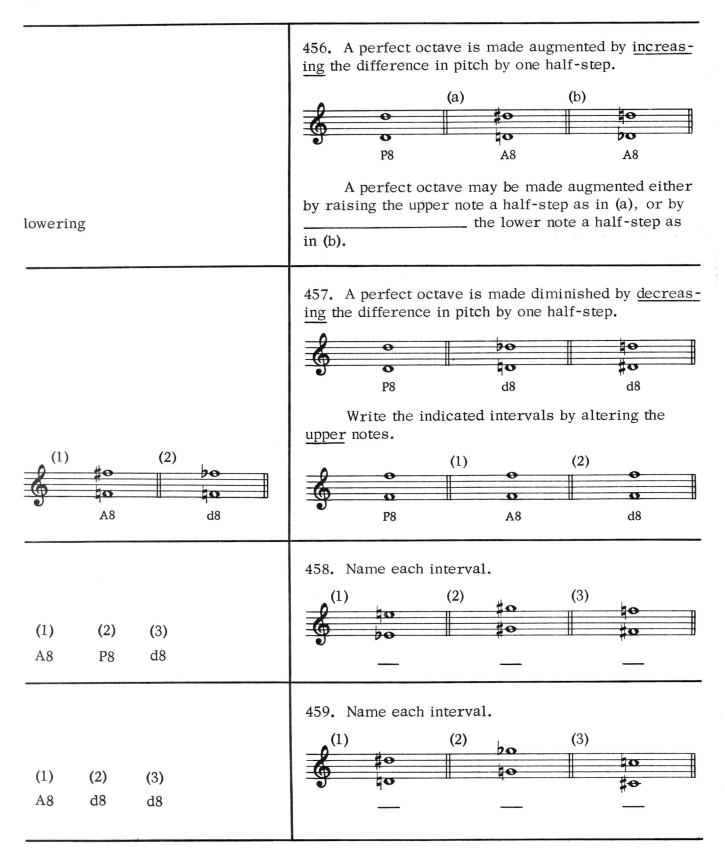

A perfect octave may be made augmented either by raising the upper note a half-step as in (a), or by _____ the lower note a half-step as in (b).

lowering

**457.** A perfect octave is made diminished by <u>decreasing</u> the difference in pitch by one half-step.

Write the indicated intervals by altering the <u>upper</u> notes.

(1)   (2)
A8    d8

**458.** Name each interval.

(1)   (2)   (3)
A8    P8    d8

**459.** Name each interval.

(1)   (2)   (3)
A8    d8    d8

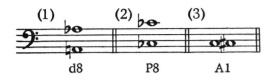

d8    P8    A1

**460.** Write the indicated intervals <u>above</u> the given notes.

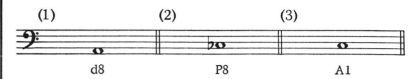

d8          P8          A1

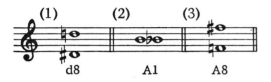

d8    A1    A8

**461.** Write the indicated intervals <u>below</u> the given notes.

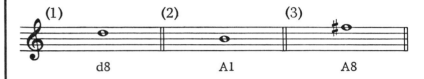

d8          A1          A8

**462.** The example below shows the basic (unaltered) 4ths.

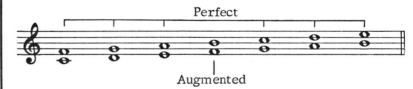

All the basic 4ths are perfect except F-B, which is augmented. How much larger is the augmented 4th F-B than the perfect 4th G-C? _____

One half-step.

**463.** The augmented 4th F-B may be made perfect by <u>reducing</u> the difference in pitch between the two tones by one half-step. Make the interval below perfect in two ways by altering first the upper, then the lower note.

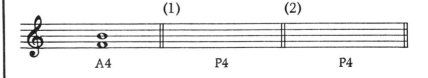

A4          P4          P4

**464.** If the basic interval is perfect, the same accidental applied to each note will cause no change in quality.

> P4        P4        P4        P4        P4

But, if the two notes are affected differently, a change of quality will occur.

> P4        d4        A4        A4

False.
*(F-B is an augmented 4th.)*

All basic 4ths are perfect.   (True/False)

_____

**465.** By referring to the quality (perfect or augmented) of the basic interval, and taking into account the effect of accidentals (if any), you should be able to analyze any 4th. *(Remember: A perfect interval made a half-step smaller is diminished; a perfect interval made a half-step larger is augmented.)*
Name each interval.

(1)        (2)        (3)

A4        P4        d4

_____    _____    _____

**466.** Name each interval.

(1)        (2)        (3)

A4        P4        A4

(1)        (2)        (3)

_____    _____    _____

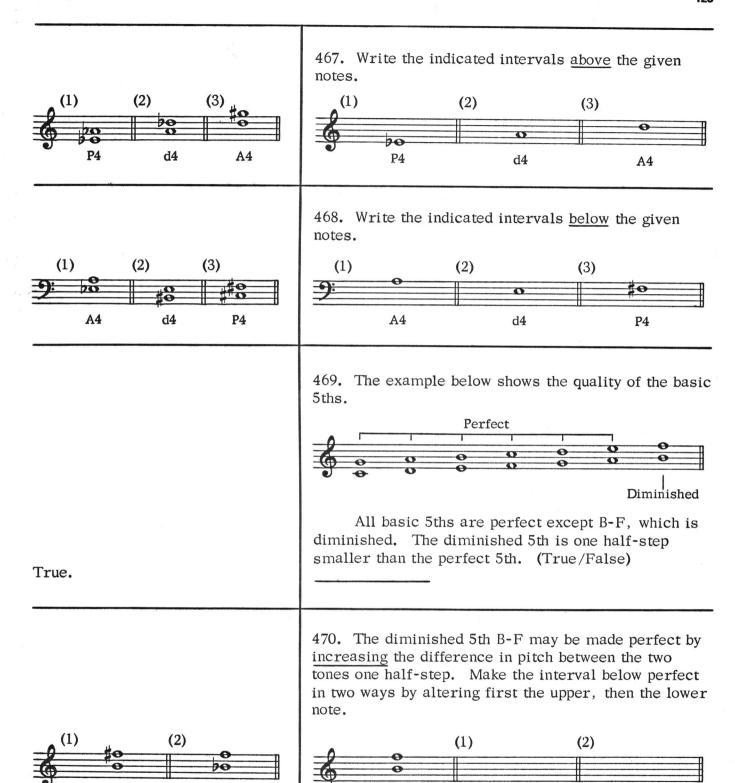

**467.** Write the indicated intervals <u>above</u> the given notes.

(1) (2) (3)

P4 d4 A4

**468.** Write the indicated intervals <u>below</u> the given notes.

(1) (2) (3)

A4 d4 P4

**469.** The example below shows the quality of the basic 5ths.

Perfect

Diminished

All basic 5ths are perfect except B-F, which is diminished. The diminished 5th is one half-step smaller than the perfect 5th. (True/False)

_____

True.

**470.** The diminished 5th B-F may be made perfect by <u>increasing</u> the difference in pitch between the two tones one half-step. Make the interval below perfect in two ways by altering first the upper, then the lower note.

(1) (2)

d5 P5 P5

(1) (2)

P5 P5

471. Make the perfect 5th below diminished in two ways by altering first the upper, then the lower note.

472. Name each interval.

473. Name each interval.

474. Write the indicated intervals <u>above</u> each note.

475. Write the indicated intervals <u>below</u> each note.

476. We shall now take up the matter of interval inversion. Knowledge of inversion is essential for the study of both harmony and counterpoint. Besides, it is useful in spelling and analyzing intervals, especially the larger ones. Only the inversion of Group I intervals will be considered now; the others are treated in Frames 514-517.

An interval is inverted by rewriting it in such a way that the upper note becomes the lower and vice versa.

Interval inversion is the process of changing the notes so that the lower becomes the _____ .

upper

477. Below is an example of interval inversion:

In (1) the original interval is inverted by writing the upper note (D) an octave lower; in (2) the lower note of the original interval is written an octave higher. The result is the same in either case.

If an interval is rewritten so that the upper note becomes the lower and vice versa, the interval is said to be _____ .

inverted

478. In both (1) and (2) in the preceding frame the displaced note was moved the interval of an octave. This is called inversion at the octave. Inversion can take place at other intervals, * but here we shall deal only with octave inversion, as it is by far the most common and useful type.

The most common interval of inversion is the

_____ .

octave

*Inversion at the 10th and 12th is encountered frequently in contrapuntal music of the 16th, 17th, and 18th centuries.

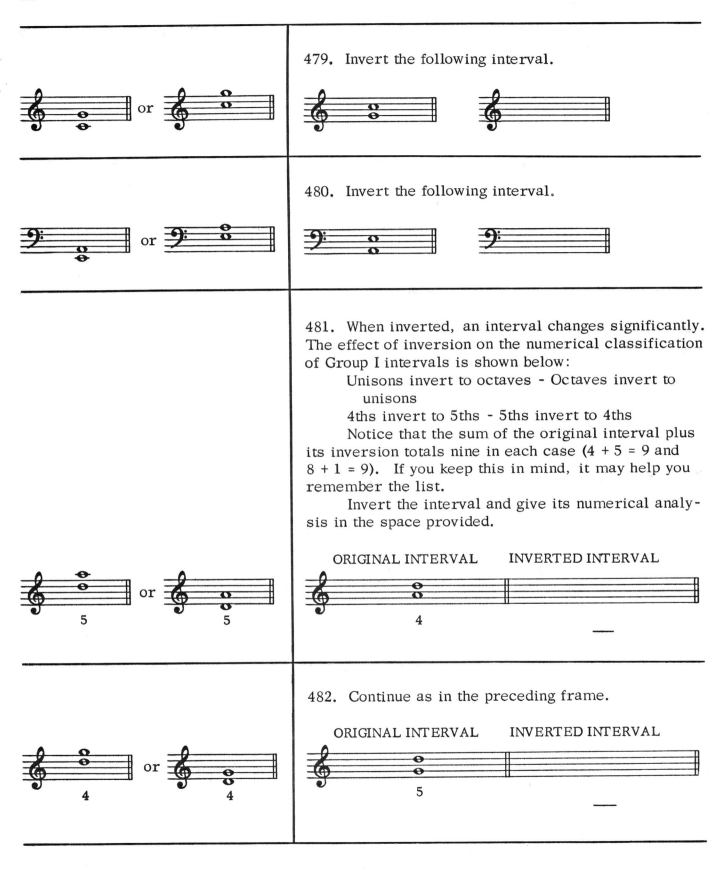

**479.** Invert the following interval.

**480.** Invert the following interval.

**481.** When inverted, an interval changes significantly. The effect of inversion on the numerical classification of Group I intervals is shown below:

Unisons invert to octaves - Octaves invert to unisons

4ths invert to 5ths - 5ths invert to 4ths

Notice that the sum of the original interval plus its inversion totals nine in each case (4 + 5 = 9 and 8 + 1 = 9). If you keep this in mind, it may help you remember the list.

Invert the interval and give its numerical analysis in the space provided.

ORIGINAL INTERVAL        INVERTED INTERVAL

**482.** Continue as in the preceding frame.

ORIGINAL INTERVAL        INVERTED INTERVAL

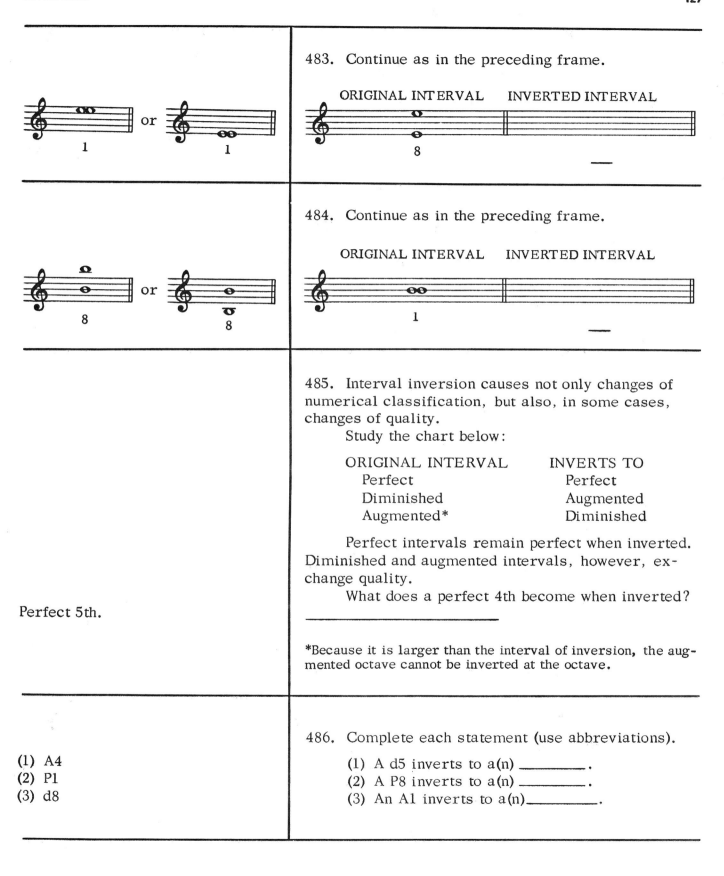

**483.** Continue as in the preceding frame.

ORIGINAL INTERVAL    INVERTED INTERVAL

8

___

**484.** Continue as in the preceding frame.

ORIGINAL INTERVAL    INVERTED INTERVAL

1

___

**485.** Interval inversion causes not only changes of numerical classification, but also, in some cases, changes of quality.

Study the chart below:

| ORIGINAL INTERVAL | INVERTS TO |
|---|---|
| Perfect | Perfect |
| Diminished | Augmented |
| Augmented* | Diminished |

Perfect intervals remain perfect when inverted. Diminished and augmented intervals, however, exchange quality.

What does a perfect 4th become when inverted?

_____

*Because it is larger than the interval of inversion, the augmented octave cannot be inverted at the octave.

Perfect 5th.

**486.** Complete each statement (use abbreviations).

(1) A d5 inverts to a(n) _____ .
(2) A P8 inverts to a(n) _____ .
(3) An A1 inverts to a(n) _____ .

(1) A4
(2) P1
(3) d8

(1) d5
(2) P4
(3) A1

**487.** Continue as in the preceding frame.

    (1) An A4 inverts to a(n) _____.
    (2) A P5 inverts to a(n) _____.
    (3) A d8 inverts to a(n) _____.

**488.** Invert each interval, and give its correct analysis.

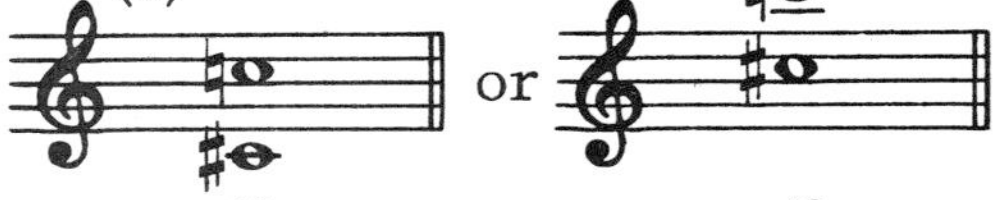

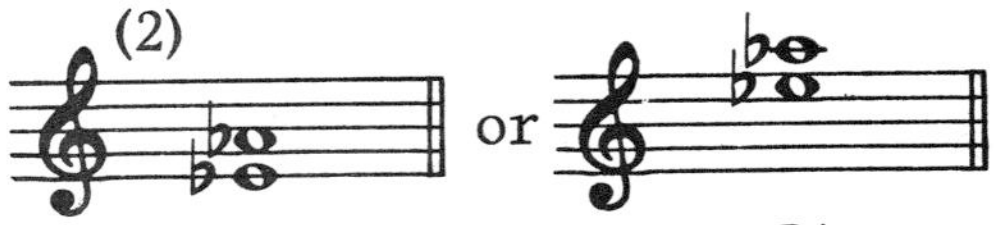

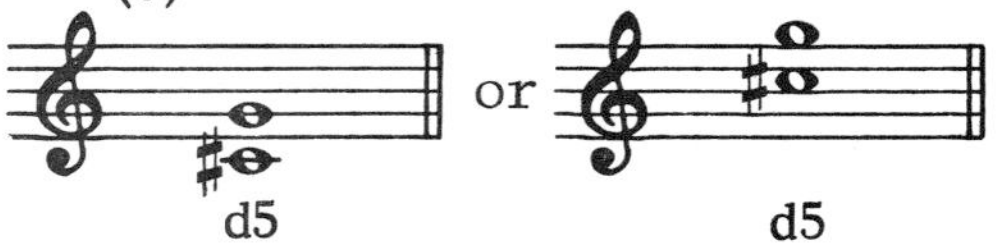

ORIGINAL      INVERTED

(1) d8 or d8

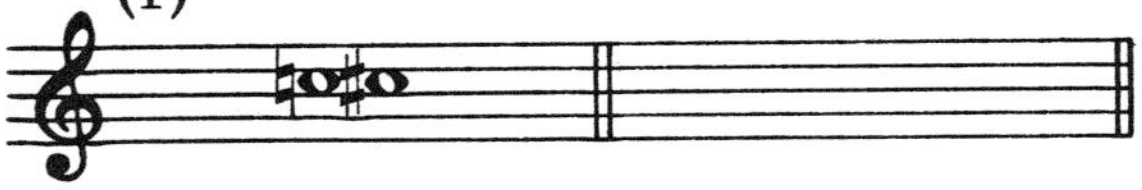

(2) P4 or P4

(3) d5 or d5

(1) A1 ___

(2) P5 ___

(3) A4 ___

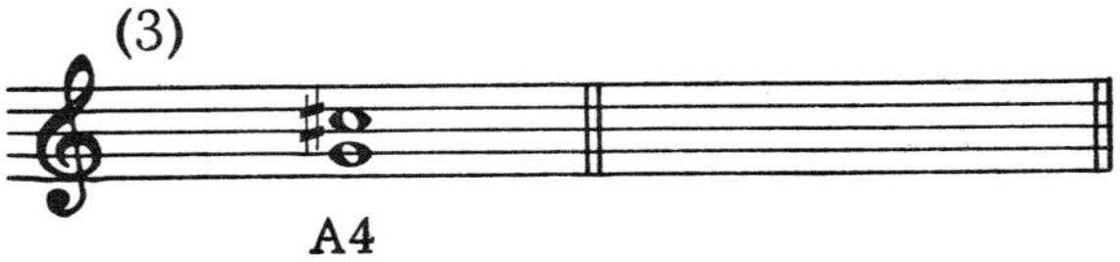

Perfect.

**489.** We shall now learn to use the terms applied to the intervals of Group II (2nds, 3rds, 6ths, and 7ths). These intervals use the terms MAJOR, MINOR, DIMINISHED, and AUGMENTED. The abbreviations for these terms are shown below:

Augmented   A
Major        M
Minor        m
Diminished  d

The intervals of both Group I and Group II use the terms diminished and augmented. Which term used by intervals of Group I is not used by those of Group II? _____

| | |
|---|---|
| major (and) minor<br>*(Any order.)* | **490.** Instead of the term perfect, the intervals of Group II use the terms _____ and _____ . |
| two | **491.** Observe the relation between the terms which apply to 2nds, 3rds, 6ths, and 7ths.<br><br>larger ——————————————→<br>d   half-step   m   half-step   M   half-step   A<br>←—————————————— smaller<br><br>The intervals of Group II have four classifications. The smallest is diminished, and the largest is augmented. A minor interval is _____ half-step(s) smaller than an augmented interval. |
| one | **492.** A major interval is made minor by decreasing its size by _____ half-step(s). |
| **(1)   (2)   (3)**<br><br>m3   M3   A3 | **493.** The interval below is a diminished 3rd. Change this interval in (1), (2), and (3) as directed. *(Apply accidentals to the upper notes only.)*<br><br>**(1)   (2)   (3)**<br><br>d3   m3   M3   A3 |
| **(1)   (2)   (3)**<br><br>m6   M6   A6 | **494.** The interval below is a diminished 6th. Change this interval in (1), (2), and (3) as directed. *(Apply accidentals to the lower notes only.)*<br><br>**(1)   (2)   (3)**<br><br>d6   m6   M6   A6 |

495. The example below shows the basic (unaltered) 2nds.

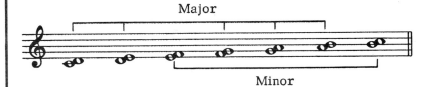

You should have little difficulty remembering the quality of basic 2nds because you have already learned that on the staff half-steps occur between the notes E-F and B-C. *It is useful to remember that a minor 2nd consists of a half-step, and a major 2nd consists of a whole-step.*

Except for E-F and B-C, all basic 2nds are

_____ .

major

496. A minor 2nd may be made major by <u>increasing</u> the difference in pitch between the two tones by one half-step. Make the interval below **major** in two ways by altering first the upper, then the lower note.

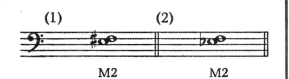

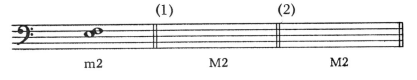

497. A major 2nd may be made minor by <u>reducing</u> the difference in pitch between the two tones by one half-step. Make the major 2nd below **minor** in two ways by altering first the upper, then the lower note.

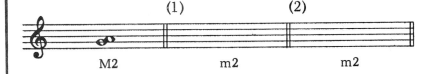

498. By referring to the quality of the basic interval, and taking into account the effect of accidentals (if any), you should be able to identify the quality of any 2nd. *(Be sure to keep in mind the chart in Frame 491.)*

   Name each interval.

   (1)          (2)          (3)

   ___          ___          ___

| (1) | (2) | (3) |
|-----|-----|-----|
| M2  | m2  | M2  |

499. Name each interval.

   (1)          (2)          (3)

   ___          ___          ___

| (1) | (2) | (3) |
|-----|-----|-----|
| M2  | A2  | m2  |

500. Name each interval.

   (1)          (2)          (3)

   ___          ___          ___

| (1) | (2) | (3) |
|-----|-----|-----|
| M2  | m2  | d2  |

501. If the diminished 2nd in (3) of the preceding frame had been written as either two C-sharps or D-flats,* the interval would have been analyzed as a _____ unison.

*Intervals which sound the same but are notated differently are called *enharmonic*. (See Frames 528-532.)

perfect

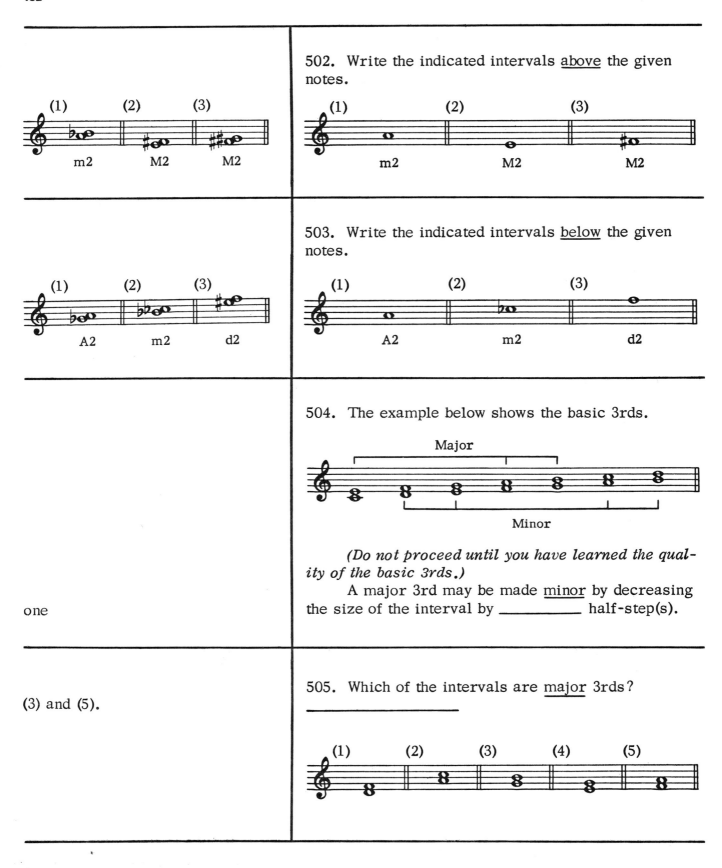

**(1)** **(2)** **(3)**

m2   M2   M2

502. Write the indicated intervals <u>above</u> the given notes.

**(1)** **(2)** **(3)**

m2        M2        M2

**(1)** **(2)** **(3)**

A2   m2   d2

503. Write the indicated intervals <u>below</u> the given notes.

**(1)** **(2)** **(3)**

A2        m2        d2

504. The example below shows the basic 3rds.

Major

Minor

*(Do not proceed until you have learned the quality of the basic 3rds.)*

A major 3rd may be made <u>minor</u> by decreasing the size of the interval by _____ half-step(s).

one

505. Which of the intervals are <u>major</u> 3rds?

_____

(3) and (5).

**(1)** **(2)** **(3)** **(4)** **(5)**

(1), (2), and (4).

506. Which of the intervals are minor 3rds?
_____

(1)      (2)      (3)      (4)      (5)

(1)   (2)   (3)   (4)

M3    M3    M3    M3

507. The intervals below are minor 3rds. Make each major by altering the upper note.

(1)          (2)          (3)          (4)

(1)      (2)      (3)

m3      m3      m3

508. The intervals below are major 3rds. Make each minor by altering the lower note.

(1)          (2)          (3)

(1)       (2)       (3)
m3        d3        M3

509. Name each interval.

(1)          (2)          (3)

___       ___       ___

(1)      (2)      (3)
M3       A3       m3

510. Name each interval.

(1)          (2)          (3)

—            —            —

(1)      (2)      (3)
m3       M3       M3

511. Name each interval.

(1)          (2)          (3)

—            —            —

(1)      (2)      (3)
M3       m3       M3

512. Write the indicated intervals <u>above</u> the given notes.

(1)          (2)          (3)

M3           m3           M3

(1)      (2)      (3)
M3       d3       m3

513. Write the indicated intervals <u>below</u> the given notes.

(1)          (2)          (3)

M3           d3           m3

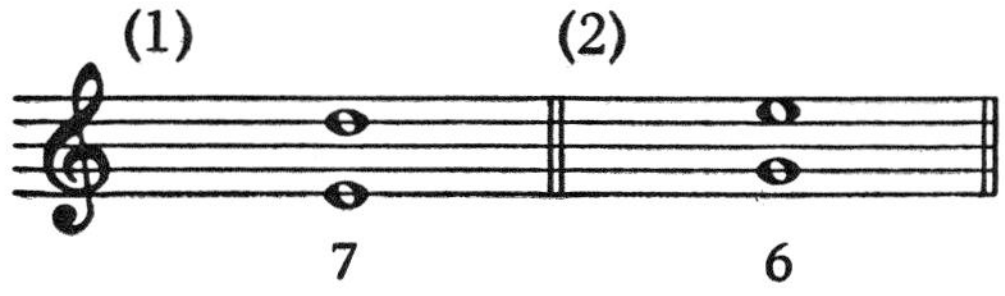

**514.** We shall make use of interval inversion to spell 6ths and 7ths. When inverted, the numerical classification of Group II intervals changes as below:

2nds invert to 7ths - 7ths invert to 2nds

3rds invert to 6ths - 6ths invert to 3rds

Invert the intervals and give their numerical classification.

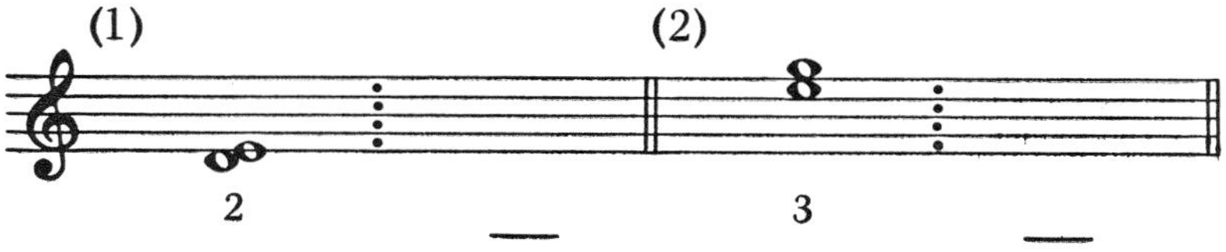

**515.** The effect of inversion on the quality of Group II intervals is shown below:

| ORIGINAL INTERVAL | INVERTS TO |
|---|---|
| Major | Minor |
| Minor | Major |
| Diminished | Augmented |
| Augmented | Diminished |

What does a major 6th become when inverted?

_____

Minor 3rd.

**516.** Complete each statement (use abbreviations).

(1) A m3 inverts to a(n) _____.

(2) A d3 inverts to a(n) _____.

(3) A M3 inverts to a(n) _____.

(1) M6
(2) A6
(3) m6

**517.** Continue as in the preceding frame.

(1) An A6 inverts to a(n) _____.

(2) A m6 inverts to a(n) _____.

(3) A d6 inverts to a(n) _____.

(1) d3
(2) M3
(3) A3

518. Now we shall see how inversions are used to spell 6ths and 7ths.  The problem in this frame is to spell a major 6th <u>above</u> the note E.

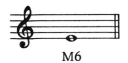

The solution is reached in two steps:  (1) identify the inversion of the desired interval (a major 6th inverts to a minor 3rd), (2) write a minor 3rd <u>below</u> the (higher) octave of the given note.

If a minor 6th had been desired, it would have been necessary to write a _____ 3rd below the (higher) octave of the given note.

major

---

519. Let us try another example.  The problem this time is to spell a minor 7th <u>below</u> the note E.

Step 1:  A m7 inverts to a _____.

M2

---

520. To complete the problem of spelling a minor 7th below E, continue with step 2:  write a major 2nd <u>above</u> the (lower) octave of the given note.

m7

(M2)          ⬆ ——Write here

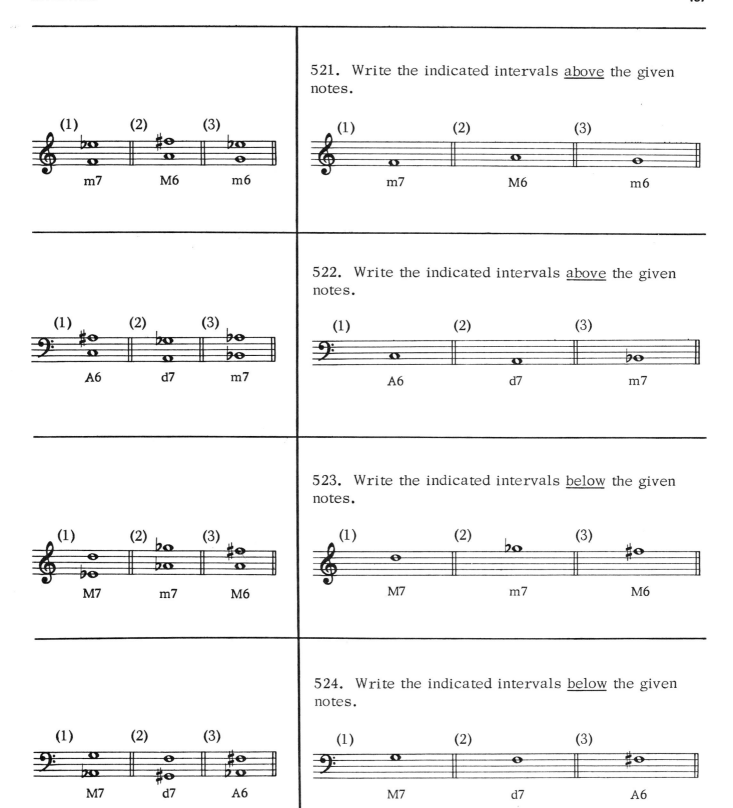

521. Write the indicated intervals <u>above</u> the given notes.

522. Write the indicated intervals <u>above</u> the given notes.

523. Write the indicated intervals <u>below</u> the given notes.

524. Write the indicated intervals <u>below</u> the given notes.

525. You may also use your knowledge of inversions to analyze an interval.  The interval E-flat to D can be identified in two steps as shown below.

Step 1:  Invert the interval.

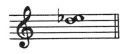

major

Step 2:  Inverted, the interval is a minor 2nd. Thus, in its original form, it must be a _____ 7th.

---

526.  Name each interval.

(1)     (2)     (3)
m7      M6      m6

---

527.  Name each interval.

(1)     (2)     (3)
d7      m7      A6

**528.** Two intervals which sound the same but are notated differently are said to be ENHARMONIC.
Name each of the intervals below.

(1) _____    (2) _____

---

(1)        (2)
A6         m7

---

enharmonic

**529.** The preceding frame shows that an augmented 6th is _____ with a minor 7th.

---

(1)        (2)
A2         m3

**530.** Apply accidentals to the notes of the second interval to make it enharmonic with the first. Also, name each interval.

(1) _____    (2) _____

---

(1)        (2)
A4         d5

**531.** Apply an accidental to one of the notes of the second interval to make it enharmonic with the first. Also, name each interval.

(1) _____    (2) _____

(1) m3
(2) d5
(3) m7

**532.** The preceding few frames have shown several enharmonic intervals. Although others are possible, the ones presented are those most frequently encountered in the study of music theory.

Complete the list below:

(1) An A2 is enharmonic with a _____ .
(2) An A4 is enharmonic with a _____ .
(3) An A6 is enharmonic with a _____ .

---

**533.** Occasionally an interval is altered to such an extent that the terms diminished and augmented do not suffice. In such a case the interval is referred to as "doubly-diminished" or "doubly-augmented."

(1) AA4          (2) dd5

two

The doubly-augmented 4th is _____ half-steps larger than the perfect 4th.

---

**534.** Write the indicated intervals <u>above</u> the given notes.

(1) AA5     (2) dd6     (3) AA4

(1) AA5     (2) dd6     (3) AA4

---

**535.** Name each interval.

(1)          (2)          (3)
A4           d3           AA5

___          ___          ___

SUMMARY

The terms used by the intervals of Groups I and II are shown below:

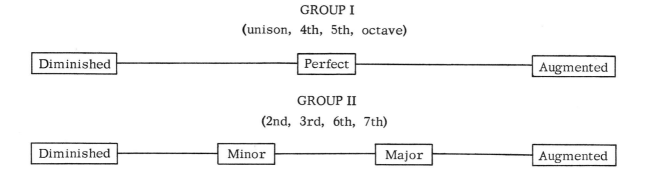

GROUP I
(unison, 4th, 5th, octave)

| Diminished | Perfect | Augmented |

GROUP II
(2nd, 3rd, 6th, 7th)

| Diminished | Minor | Major | Augmented |

Group I intervals have three possible categories whereas Group II intervals have four. The term diminished represents the smallest interval. Each successive term (left-to-right) represents an increase in size of one half-step.

In addition to its importance for more advanced theory study, knowledge of interval inversion may be used to spell larger intervals such as 6ths and 7ths. When inverted, the numerical classification and the quality of intervals change in the following manner:

| ORIGINAL | INVERTED |
|----------|----------|
| Perfect | Perfect |
| Major | Minor |
| Minor | Major |
| Augmented | Diminished |
| Diminished | Augmented |
| | |
| Unison | Octave |
| 2nd | 7th |
| 3rd | 6th |
| 4th | 5th |
| 5th | 4th |
| 6th | 3rd |
| 7th | 2nd |
| Octave | Unison |

# 7
# The Basic Scales

The word _scale_ is derived from the Latin, _scala_, which means "ladder." It refers to an orderly ascending or descending arrangement of successive pitches within the limit of an octave. There are many kinds of scales depending on the intervallic relation of the notes. This chapter is concerned with the scales formed by only the seven basic (unaltered) notes. Because no accidentals are used, these are called _basic_ _scales_.

| | |
|---|---|
| | 536. A stepwise arrangement of the tones contained in one octave is called a SCALE. By "stepwise" is meant an alphabetical arrangement of the letters which represent tones. |
| | Write the letters which produce a stepwise series of tones starting and ending on A. |
| A B C D E F G A | ___ ___ ___ ___ ___ ___ ___ ___ |
| | 537. Write the letters representing a stepwise series of tones starting and ending on E. |
| E F G A B C D E | ___ ___ ___ ___ ___ ___ ___ ___ |
| | 538. In a SCALE the tones contained in one octave are organized stepwise. In a stepwise series of tones, the letters representing the sounds appear in |
| alphabetical | _____ order. |

539. A stepwise arrangement of tones is also said to be DIATONIC. To form a diatonic scale, all of the seven basic notes must be present plus the octave duplication of the first note. Thus, eight notes are required to form a diatonic scale. Also, the notes must be stated in alphabetical order; none may be repeated (except for the octave duplication of the first note), and none may be omitted.

How many notes are needed to form a diatonic scale? _____

Eight.

540. The CHROMATIC scale arranges <u>all</u> of the sounds contained in one octave (in the system of equal temperament), and consists of thirteen tones (including the octave duplication of the first tone).

Other scales are limited to eight tones (including the octave duplication of the first tone). These are called DIATONIC scales.

All of the tones normally contained in one octave are included in the _____ scale.

*Play the chromatic scale at the piano from C up to C. Note that all the intervals are half-steps. Sing the same scale.*

chromatic

541. Scales which utilize only basic (unaltered) notes are called BASIC scales.

Write the letters representing the basic scale starting on C.

__ __ __ __ __ __ __ __

C D E F G A B C

542. Write on the staff the <u>basic</u> scale starting on F.

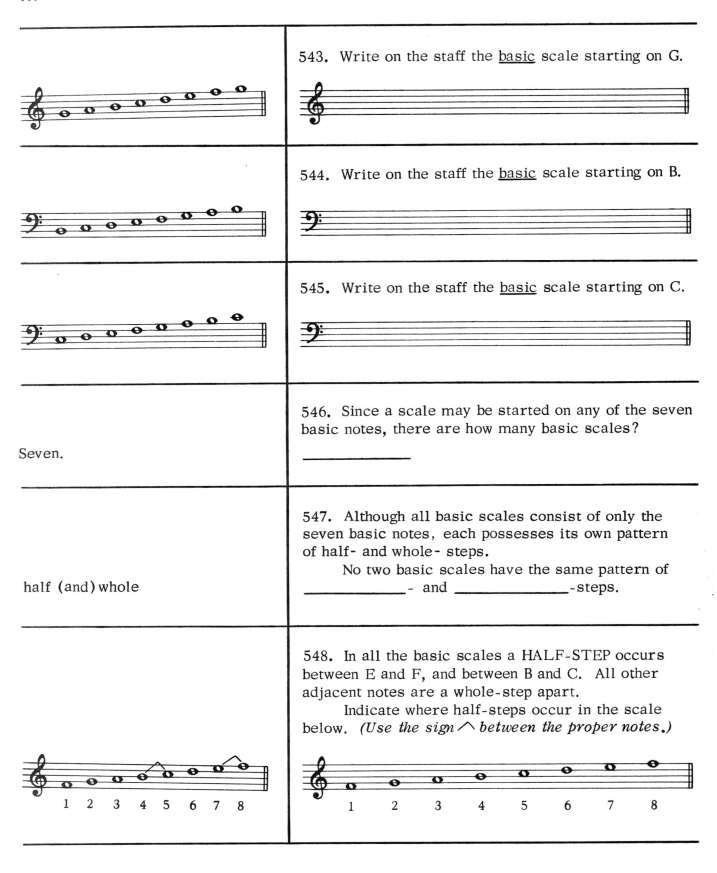

**543.** Write on the staff the <u>basic</u> scale starting on G.

**544.** Write on the staff the <u>basic</u> scale starting on B.

**545.** Write on the staff the <u>basic</u> scale starting on C.

**546.** Since a scale may be started on any of the seven basic notes, there are how many basic scales?

_____

Seven.

**547.** Although all basic scales consist of only the seven basic notes, each possesses its own pattern of half- and whole- steps.

No two basic scales have the same pattern of

_____ - and _____ -steps.

half (and) whole

**548.** In all the basic scales a HALF-STEP occurs between E and F, and between B and C. All other adjacent notes are a whole-step apart.

Indicate where half-steps occur in the scale below. *(Use the sign ⌃ between the proper notes.)*

1   2   3   4   5   6   7   8

1      2      3      4      5      6      7      8

**549.** Note in the preceding frame that the notes of the scale are numbered from 1 to 8 beginning with the lowest note. Thus we can say that, in the basic scale starting on F, half-steps occur between the 4th and 5th and between the 7th and 8th degrees.

Indicate where half-steps occur in the scale below. *(Use the sign ⌃ between the proper notes.)*

---

1st - 2nd
5th - 6th

**550.** Between which degrees do half-steps occur in the scale below? _____ and ____; _____ and _____.

---

3rd - 4th
6th - 7th

**551.** Between which degrees do half-steps occur in the scale below? _____ and ____; _____ and ____.

---

3rd - 4th
7th - 8th

**552.** Between which degrees do half-steps occur in the scale below? _____ and _____; _____ and _____.

Seven.

553. Due to the pattern of half- and whole-steps, each basic scale has its own unique intervallic structure. For this reason no two basic scales sound alike.

When tonal material is limited to the basic notes, how many scales are possible? _____

*Sing, or play at the piano the seven basic scales. Note the effect that each scale has because of its particular pattern of half- and whole-steps.*

---

D

554. Each of the basic scales has a modal name. *

| Basic Scale | Modal Name |
|-------------|------------|
| A B C D E F G A | *Aeolian* |
| B C D E F G A B | *Locrian* |
| C D E F G A B C | *Ionian* |
| D E F G A B C D | *Dorian* |
| E F G A B C D E | *Phrygian* |
| F G A B C D E F | *Lydian* |
| G A B C D E F G | *Mixolydian* |

The DORIAN mode is the same as the basic scale starting on the note _____.

*Study the list of modal names above before continuing with the next frame.*

*These names are derived from tonal structures known as the Church modes. Dorian, Phrygian, Lydian, and Mixolydian date from about the 8th century. Ionian and Aeolian were added to the system by the theorist Glareanus in his treatise *Dodekachordon* (1547). The Locrian mode existed at this time merely as a theoretical possibility. The Church modes served as the tonal basis of Western music until about 1600, after which time they were gradually modified to form the major-minor tonal system which is the basis of most of the music heard today.

Ionian.

555. You must not think that modal scales can be written only with basic (unaltered) notes. By using accidentals, any mode can be constructed on any pitch. But learning to associate the various modes with their equivalent basic scale can serve as a useful point of reference when transposition to other pitches is desired. Our concern here is that you appreciate the variety of scale structures available with merely the seven basic notes.

What is the modal name of the basic scale starting on C? _____

---

A

556. The AEOLIAN mode is the same as the basic scale starting on the note _____.

---

E

557. The PHRYGIAN mode is the same as the basic scale starting on the note _____.

---

C

558. The IONIAN mode is the same as the basic scale starting on the note _____.

---

Lydian.

559. What is the modal name of the basic scale starting on F? _____

Dorian.

**560.** What is the modal name of the basic scale starting on D? _____

---

Mixolydian.

**561.** What is the modal name of the basic scale starting on G? _____

---

Locrian.

**562.** What is the modal name of the basic scale starting on B? _____

---

**563.** Write the DORIAN mode. *(Use basic notes only.)*

---

**564.** Write the MIXOLYDIAN mode. *(Use basic notes only.)*

---

**565.** Write the PHRYGIAN mode. *(Use basic notes only.)*

**566.** Write the LOCRIAN mode. *(Use basic notes only.)*

**567.** Write the LYDIAN mode. *(Use basic notes only.)*

**568.** Write the IONIAN mode. *(Use basic notes only.)*

**569.** Write the AEOLIAN mode. *(Use basic notes only.)*

4th - 5th
7th - 8th

**570.** In the LYDIAN mode a half-step occurs between the _____ and _____ degrees, and between the _____ and _____ degrees. *(You may refer to the scale you have written in Frame 567.)*

3rd - 4th
7th - 8th

**571.** In the IONIAN mode a half-step occurs between the _____ and _____ degrees, and between the _____ and _____ degrees. *(You may refer to the scale you have written in Frame 568.)*

| | |
|---|---|
| 1st - 2nd<br>5th - 6th | 572. In the PHRYGIAN mode a half-step occurs between the _____ and _____ degrees, and between the _____ and _____ degrees. *(You may refer to the scale you have written in Frame 565.)* |
| D | 573. The first and last note of a scale is called the KEYNOTE.* The keynote of the <u>Dorian</u> mode (as you have written it in Frame 563) is _____.<br><br>*The keynote is also called the "tonic-note," or "key-center." |
| G. | 574. What is the keynote of the <u>Mixolydian</u> mode (as you have written it in Frame 564)?<br><br>_____ |
| G. | 575. What is the keynote of the basic scale whose 3rd degree is B? _____ |
| E. | 576. What is the keynote of the basic scale whose 4th degree is A? _____ |
| D. | 577. What is the keynote of the basic scale whose 7th degree is C? _____ |
| A. | 578. What is the keynote of the basic scale whose 6th degree is F? _____ |

| | |
|---|---|
| E. | 579. What is the keynote of the basic scale whose 5th degree is B? _____ |
| keynote | 580. The note upon which a scale begins and ends is called the _____. |

## SUMMARY

A basic scale may be constructed on each of the seven basic notes. Thus there are seven basic scales. No two of these sound alike because the pattern of half- and whole-steps is different in each case. Basic scales are sometimes identified by their modal names. These are shown below:

Basic scale starting on A - Aeolian
Basic scale starting on B - Locrian
Basic scale starting on C - Ionian
Basic scale starting on D - Dorian
Basic scale starting on E - Phrygian
Basic scale starting on F - Lydian
Basic scale starting on G - Mixolydian

# 8
# The Major Scale

The basic scale based on the note C is called the Ionian mode. It is also called the "C major scale" and is probably the most familiar of all scale structures. In this chapter you will learn to write major scales on any note by applying accidentals to produce the requisite pattern of half- and whole-steps.

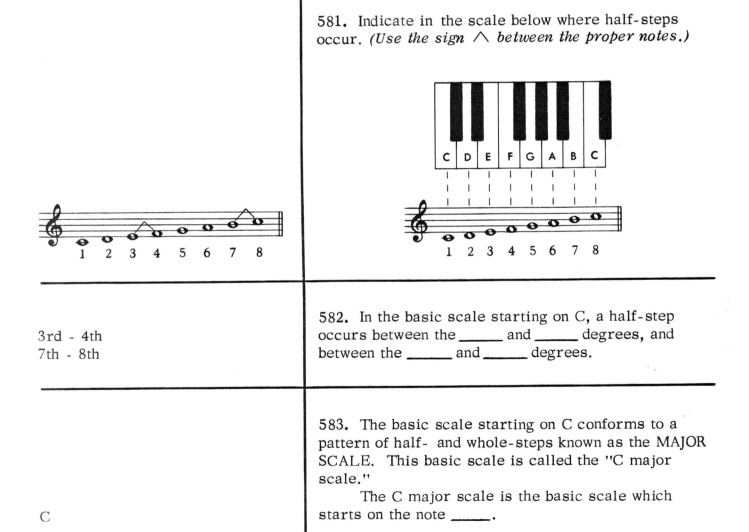

**581.** Indicate in the scale below where half-steps occur. *(Use the sign ∧ between the proper notes.)*

3rd - 4th
7th - 8th

**582.** In the basic scale starting on C, a half-step occurs between the _____ and _____ degrees, and between the _____ and _____ degrees.

C

**583.** The basic scale starting on C conforms to a pattern of half- and whole-steps known as the MAJOR SCALE. This basic scale is called the "C major scale."

The C major scale is the basic scale which starts on the note _____.

**584.** The major scale may be represented as a series of steps, as below:

H = Half-step
W = Whole-step

*Sing this scale saying the numbers of the degrees. Be careful to sing a half-step between 3 and 4 and between 7 and 8.*

The major scale is the same as the (Dorian/ Aeolian/Ionian) mode. _____

Ionian.

**585.** A major scale may start on any note. However, whole-steps must occur between all adjacent notes except the _____ and _____, and the _____ and _____ degrees.

3rd - 4th
7th - 8th

**586.** What interval occurs between the 3rd and 4th, and 7th and 8th degrees of the major scale? The _____-step.

half

**587.** Which of the scales below is a major scale?

_____

(2).

(1).

588. Which of the scales below is a major scale?

_____

(1)

(2)

(2).

589. Which of the scales below is a major scale?

_____

(1)

(2)

590. Scale (2) in the preceding frame shows that a major scale may start on an altered note as well as a basic note. This scale is called the "G-flat major scale" because the first and last notes are G-flat. Bear in mind that the words "sharp" or "flat" are included in the name of the scale only when the first note (keynote) is sharped or flatted.

What is the keynote of the F-sharp major scale?

F-sharp.

_____

**591.** Add accidentals to form the F major scale.

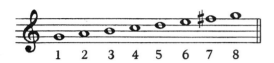

**592.** Add accidentals to form the G major scale.

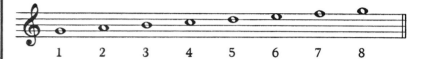

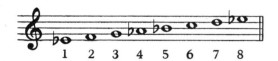

**593.** Add accidentals to form the E-flat major scale.

**594.** Add accidentals to form the D major scale.

**595.** Add accidentals to form the B-flat major scale.

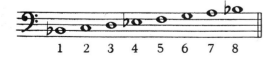

596. Add accidentals to form the A major scale.

597. Add accidentals to form the A-flat major scale.

598. Write the E major scale.

599. Write the D-flat major scale.

600. Write the F-sharp major scale.

601. Write the G-flat major scale.

602. Write the B major scale.

603. Write the C-sharp major scale.

604. Write the C-flat major scale.

C

605. The basic scale which conforms to the pattern of half- and whole-steps of the major scale begins and ends on the note _____.

| | |
|---|---|
| True. | 606. All adjacent scale degrees in the major scale are separated by either a whole-step or a half-step. (True/False) _____ |
| False. *(Half-steps occur between 3-4, and 7-8 in the major scale.)* | 607. In the major scale a half-step occurs between the 3rd and 4th, and between the 6th and 7th degrees. (True/False) _____ |
| B-flat. | 608. What accidental must be added to the <u>Lydian</u> mode (F up to F) to form a major scale?_____ |
| F-sharp. | 609. What accidental must be added to the <u>Mixolydian</u> mode (G up to G) to form a major scale?_____ |
| E major. | 610. F-sharp is the second degree of what major scale? _____ |
| G-flat major. | 611. B-flat is the third degree of what major scale? _____ |
| A-flat major. | 612. D-flat is the fourth degree of what major scale? _____ |

E major.

613. B‚is the fifth degree of what major scale?

_____

---

F major.

614. D is the sixth degree of what major scale?

_____

---

D major.

615. C-sharp is the seventh degree of what major scale? _____

---

616. You may find it helpful to regard the major scale as consisting of two groups of four notes each called TETRACHORDS.

D MAJOR SCALE — upper tetrachord — lower tetrachord

Examine the succession of intervals contained in each tetrachord. The lower tetrachord consists of two whole-steps followed by a half-step; the upper tetrachord consists of _____

_____.

two whole-steps followed by a half-step.
(_Or equivalent._)

whole

617. The example in the preceding frame shows that the upper, and lower tetrachords of the major scale contain the same succession of intervals (two whole-steps followed by a half-step). The interval separating the two tetrachords is a (half/whole) _____ -step.

618. Write the lower tetrachord of the A-flat major scale.

619. Write the upper tetrachord of the A-flat major scale. *(Remember: the first note of the upper tetrachord is a whole-step above the last note of the lower.)*

Lower: C
Upper: F

620. Any tetrachord consisting of two whole-steps followed by a half-step may be either the upper or lower tetrachord of a major scale. The tetrachord C D E F is the lower tetrachord of the _____ major scale, and also the upper tetrachord of the _____ major scale.

Lower: B
Upper: E

621. The tetrachord below is the lower tetrachord of the _____ major scale, and also the upper tetrachord of the _____ major scale.

| | |
|---|---|
| C | 622. The lower tetrachord of the G major scale is the same as the upper tetrachord of the _____ major scale. |
| A | 623. The upper tetrachord of the D major scale is the same as the lower tetrachord of the _____ major scale. |

SUMMARY

A tetrachord is a four-note scale pattern. Two tetrachords combine to make a scale. For major scales, both the upper and lower tetrachords contain the same intervals: two whole-steps followed by a half-step. Any tetrachord which has this pattern may be either the upper or lower tetrachord of a major scale. In major scales, a whole-step separates the upper from the lower tetrachord. Considered as a whole, the major scale consists of whole-steps, except for half-steps between the 3rd and 4th, and the 7th and 8th degrees. By using accidentals to produce this pattern, a major scale can be constructed on any note.

# 9
# The Minor Scales

Three types of minor scales are presented in this chapter: <u>natural</u>, <u>harmonic</u>, and <u>melodic</u>. Each of these has a different pattern of half- and whole-steps and will be treated separately. In actual music, however, it is unusual for a composition to be based exclusively on a single minor scale type. Melodic and harmonic resources usually are drawn from all three, resulting in much greater tonal variety than is available in the major scale.

---

2nd - 3rd
5th - 6th

---

**624.** Indicate in the scale below where half-steps occur. *(Use the sign* ∧ *between the proper notes.)*

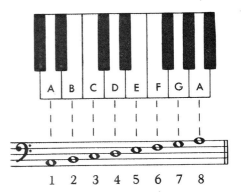

**625.** In the basic scale starting on the note A, half-steps occur between the _____ and _____ degrees, and between the _____ and _____ degrees.

626. The basic scale starting on the note A conforms to the pattern of half- and whole-steps of the NATURAL minor scale. *

The natural minor scale may be represented as a series of steps, as below:

H = Half-step
W = Whole-step

*Sing the natural minor scale. Be careful to observe the correct pattern of half- and whole-steps.*

The natural minor scale is the same as the basic scale starting on the note _____.

*The natural minor scale is also called the <u>pure</u>, <u>normal</u>, or <u>Aeolian</u> minor.

---

A

---

627. Between which scale degrees do half-steps occur in the natural minor scale? _____ and _____; _____ and _____.

---

2nd - 3rd
5th - 6th

---

628. The natural minor scale is the same as the _____ mode.

---

Aeolian

---

629. There are three types of minor scales: (1) harmonic minor, (2) melodic minor, and (3) _____ minor.

---

natural

(2).

630. Which of the scales below is a natural minor scale? _____

(1)

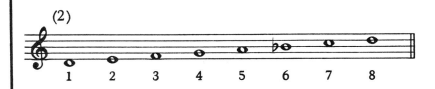

(2)

(1).

631. Which of the scales below is a natural minor scale? _____

(1)

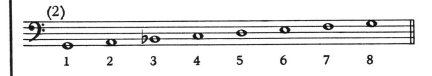

(2)

632. The <u>lower</u> tetrachord of the C natural minor scale is notated below.  Analyze the intervals contained in this tetrachord as indicated.

    W = whole-step
    H = half-step

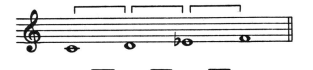

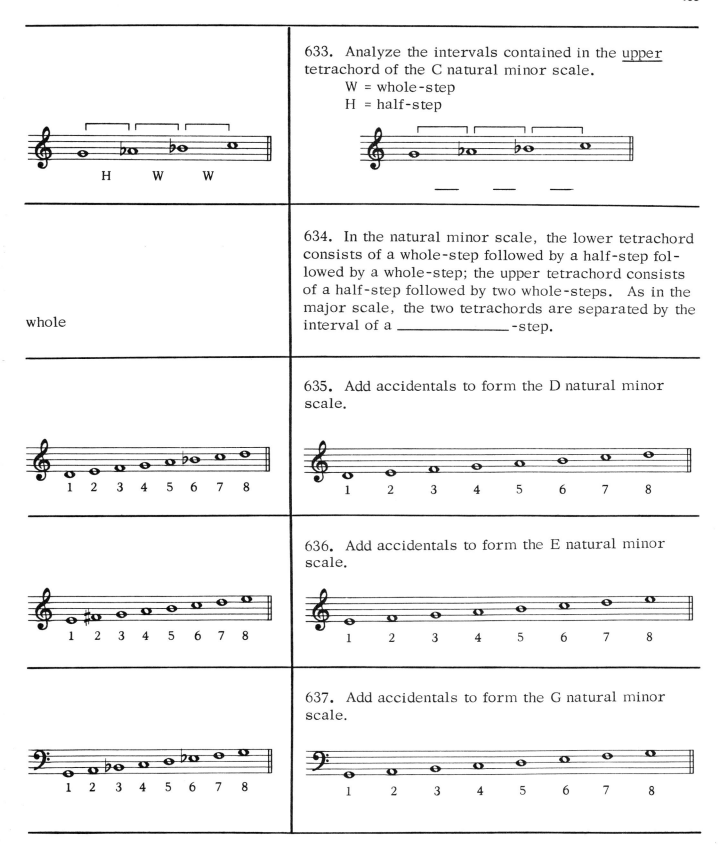

**633.** Analyze the intervals contained in the <u>upper</u> tetrachord of the C natural minor scale.

W = whole-step

H = half-step

**634.** In the natural minor scale, the lower tetrachord consists of a whole-step followed by a half-step followed by a whole-step; the upper tetrachord consists of a half-step followed by two whole-steps. As in the major scale, the two tetrachords are separated by the interval of a _____ -step.

whole

**635.** Add accidentals to form the D natural minor scale.

**636.** Add accidentals to form the E natural minor scale.

**637.** Add accidentals to form the G natural minor scale.

638. Add accidentals to form the B natural minor scale.

639. Write the F-sharp natural minor scale.

640. Write the C natural minor scale.

641. Write the C-sharp natural minor scale.

642. Write the F natural minor scale.

643. The HARMONIC MINOR SCALE has half-steps between the 2nd and 3rd, 5th and 6th, and 7th and 8th degrees.

How many half-steps are contained in the HARMONIC MINOR SCALE?_____

Three.

---

644. What is the interval separating the 6th and 7th degrees of the harmonic minor scale?

_____

*(Refer to the scale in the preceding frame.)*

Augmented 2nd.

---

645. A unique feature of the harmonic minor scale is the augmented 2nd which occurs between the 6th and 7th degrees. The augmented 2nd is the same as a whole-step plus a _____-step.

half

---

646. Show the degrees between which half-steps occur in the harmonic minor scale.

_____ and _____ ; _____ and _____ ; _____ and _____ .

2nd (and) 3rd
5th (and) 6th
7th (and) 8th

647. The harmonic minor scale may be represented
as a series of steps, as below:

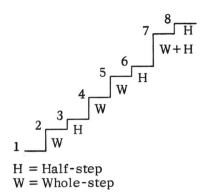

H = Half-step
W = Whole-step

*Sing the harmonic minor scale. Be careful to observe
the correct pattern of half- and whole-steps.*

In the harmonic minor scale, half-steps occur
between the 2nd and 3rd, 5th and 6th, and 7th and 8th
degrees. The interval between the 6th and 7th degrees
is a step-and-a-half. The remaining intervals are all
_____-steps.

whole

---

648. Is the scale below a harmonic minor scale?
_____

Yes.

---

649. Is the scale below a harmonic minor scale?
_____

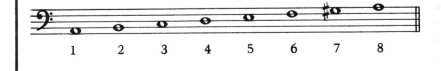

Yes.

| | |
|---|---|
| No. | **650.** Is the scale below a harmonic minor scale? _____ |
| Natural minor. | **651.** What type of scale is shown in the preceding frame? _____ |
| | **652.** Rewrite the scale in Frame 650 so that it is a C harmonic minor scale. |
| The 7th scale degree was raised a half-step. | **653.** As originally written, the scale in Frame 650 was a natural minor scale. What alteration was necessary to transform it into a harmonic minor scale? _____ _____ |
| half | **654.** The harmonic minor scale differs from the natural minor scale only in that the 7th degree is raised a _____ -step. |

**655.** To write a harmonic minor scale: (1) write a natural minor scale; (2) raise the 7th degree a half-step.

Transform the natural minor scale below into a harmonic minor scale in the manner described above.

**656.** Transform the natural minor scale below into a harmonic minor scale.

**657.** Add accidentals to form the D harmonic minor scale *(Check all intervals.)*

**658.** Add accidentals to form the E harmonic minor scale. *(Check all intervals.)*

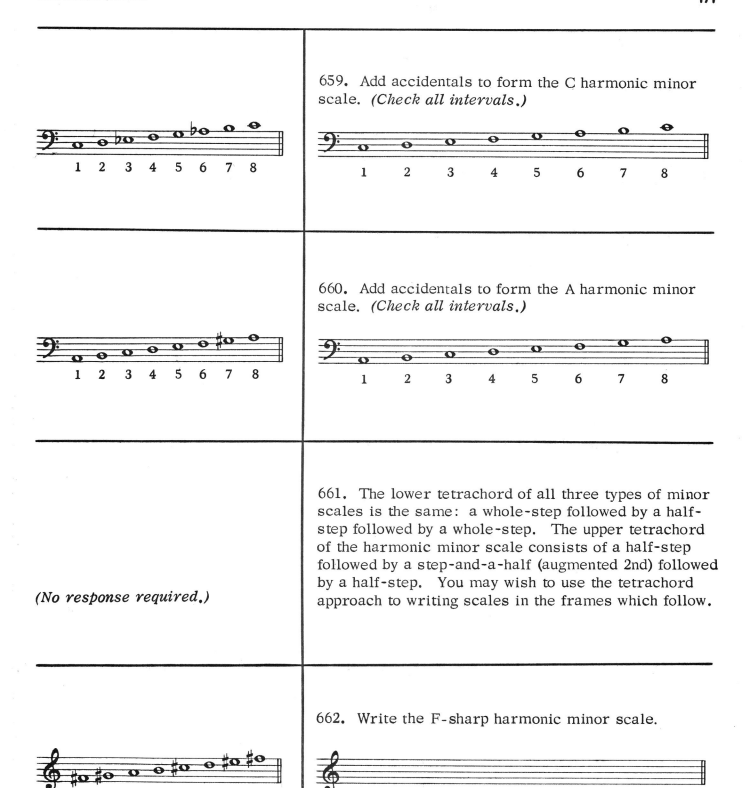

**659.** Add accidentals to form the C harmonic minor scale. *(Check all intervals.)*

**660.** Add accidentals to form the A harmonic minor scale. *(Check all intervals.)*

**661.** The lower tetrachord of all three types of minor scales is the same: a whole-step followed by a half-step followed by a whole-step. The upper tetrachord of the harmonic minor scale consists of a half-step followed by a step-and-a-half (augmented 2nd) followed by a half-step. You may wish to use the tetrachord approach to writing scales in the frames which follow.

*(No response required.)*

**662.** Write the F-sharp harmonic minor scale.

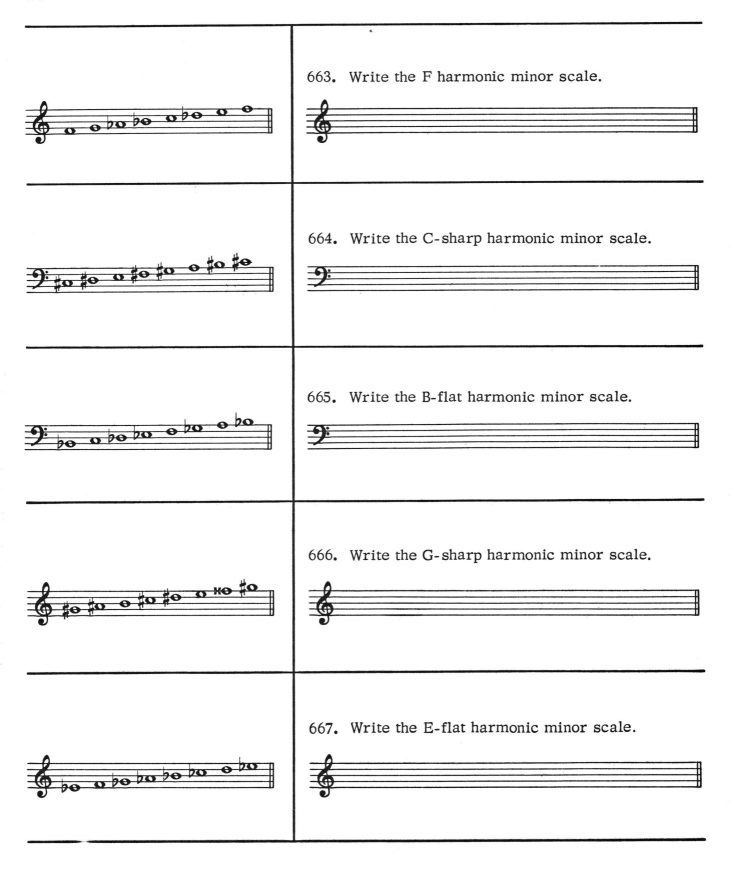

663. Write the F harmonic minor scale.

664. Write the C-sharp harmonic minor scale.

665. Write the B-flat harmonic minor scale.

666. Write the G-sharp harmonic minor scale.

667. Write the E-flat harmonic minor scale.

**668.** Write the D-sharp harmonic minor scale.

**669.** Write the A-flat harmonic minor scale.

**670.** Write the A-sharp harmonic minor scale.

natural

**671.** The minor scale which has half-steps between the 2nd and 3rd and the 5th and 6th degrees is called the _____ minor scale.

harmonic

**672.** The minor scale which has half-steps between the 2nd and 3rd, 5th and 6th, and 7th and 8th degrees is called the _____ minor scale.

melodic

**673.** In all the scales studied to this point the ascending and descending forms have contained the same notes. The MELODIC MINOR SCALE, however, has one pattern of half- and whole-steps for its ascending form and another for its descending form.

The only scale which has different patterns of half- and whole-steps for its ascending and descending forms is called the _____ minor scale.

674. Indicate where half-steps occur in the scale below. *(Use the sign ∧ between the proper notes.)*

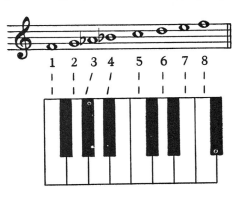

2nd - 3rd
7th - 8th

675. The scale above is the ASCENDING form of the F melodic minor scale.

In the <u>ascending</u> form of the melodic minor scale, half-steps occur between the _____ and _____, and the _____ and _____ degrees. *(Refer to the scale in the preceding frame.)*

melodic

676. The <u>ascending</u> form of the melodic minor scale may be represented as a series of steps, as below:

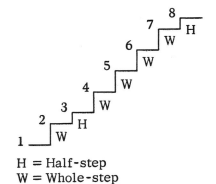

H = Half-step
W = Whole-step

*Sing the <u>ascending</u> form of the melodic minor scale. Be careful to observe the correct pattern of half- and whole-steps.*

Any scale which has a half-step between the 2nd and 3rd degrees, and between the 7th and 8th degrees corresponds to the pattern of half- and whole-steps known as the ASCENDING form of the _____ minor scale.

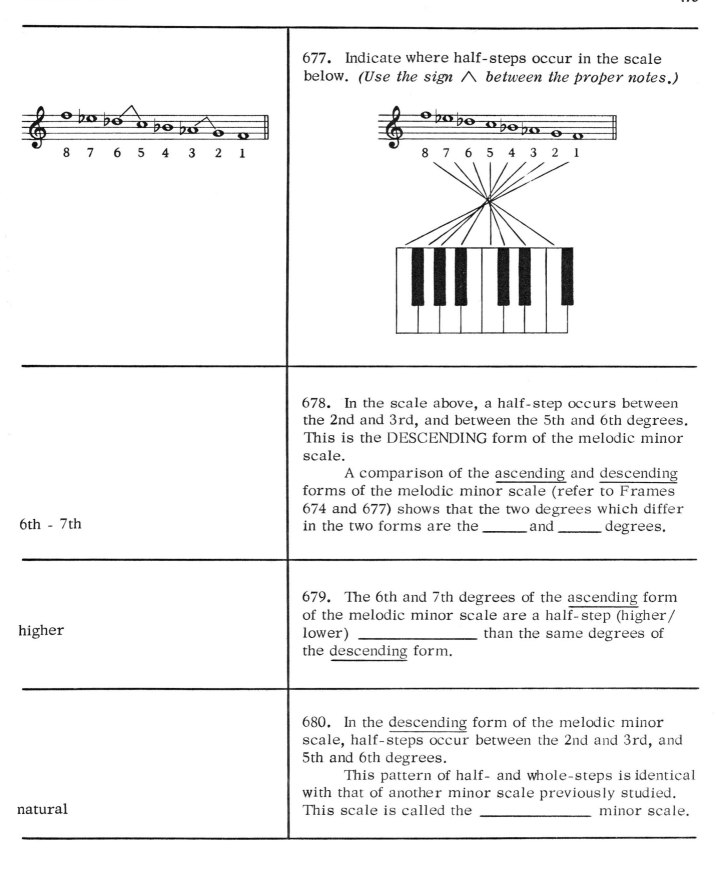

**677.** Indicate where half-steps occur in the scale below. *(Use the sign ∧ between the proper notes.)*

8 7 6 5 4 3 2 1

**678.** In the scale above, a half-step occurs between the 2nd and 3rd, and between the 5th and 6th degrees. This is the DESCENDING form of the melodic minor scale.

A comparison of the <u>ascending</u> and <u>descending</u> forms of the melodic minor scale (refer to Frames 674 and 677) shows that the two degrees which differ in the two forms are the _____ and _____ degrees.

6th - 7th

**679.** The 6th and 7th degrees of the <u>ascending</u> form of the melodic minor scale are a half-step (higher/ lower) _____ than the same degrees of the <u>descending</u> form.

higher

**680.** In the <u>descending</u> form of the melodic minor scale, half-steps occur between the 2nd and 3rd, and 5th and 6th degrees.

This pattern of half- and whole-steps is identical with that of another minor scale previously studied. This scale is called the _____ minor scale.

natural

681. The descending form of the melodic minor scale may be represented as a series of steps, as below:

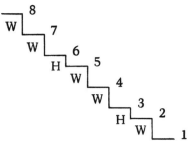

H = Half-step
W = Whole-step

*Sing the <u>descending</u> form of the melodic minor scale. Be careful to observe the correct pattern of half- and whole-steps.*

The pattern of half- and whole-steps in the natural minor scale is the same as that of the _____ form of the <u>melodic</u> minor scale.

descending

---

(1).

682. Which of the scales below is the <u>descending</u> form of the D melodic minor scale? _____

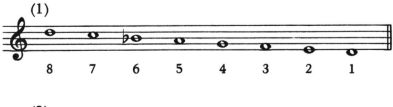

(1)

8  7  6  5  4  3  2  1

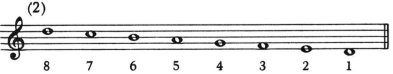

(2)

8  7  6  5  4  3  2  1

(2).

**683.** Which of the scales below is the <u>ascending</u> form of the C-sharp melodic minor scale?_____

(1)

1   2   3   4   5   6   7   8

(2)

1   2   3   4   5   6   7   8

(2).

**684.** Which of the scales below is the <u>ascending</u> form of the G melodic minor scale? _____

(1)

1   2   3   4   5   6   7   8

(2)

1   2   3   4   5   6   7   8

Major.

**685.** Scale 1 in the preceding frame is what type of scale?_____

The 3rd.

686. Compare Scale 1 with Scale 2 in Frame 684. What scale degree is different? _____

half

687. The ASCENDING form of the melodic minor scale is the same as a major scale, except that the 3rd degree is a _____-step lower.

True.

688. The lower tetrachord of all three types of minor scales consists of a whole-step followed by a half-step followed by a whole-step. In the melodic minor scale, the ascending upper tetrachord is the same as in the major scale (whole-step, whole-step, half-step); the descending upper tetrachord is the same as in the natural minor scale (half-step, whole-step, whole-step).

The tetrachord below is the upper tetrachord of the B melodic minor scale, ascending form. (True/False) _____

689. Write the upper tetrachord of the D melodic minor scale, descending form.

690. Write the upper tetrachord of the E melodic minor scale, ascending form.

691. Use accidentals to form the C melodic minor scale.

(ASCENDING FORM)

(DESCENDING FORM)

692. Use accidentals to form the F melodic minor scale.

(ASCENDING FORM)

(DESCENDING FORM)

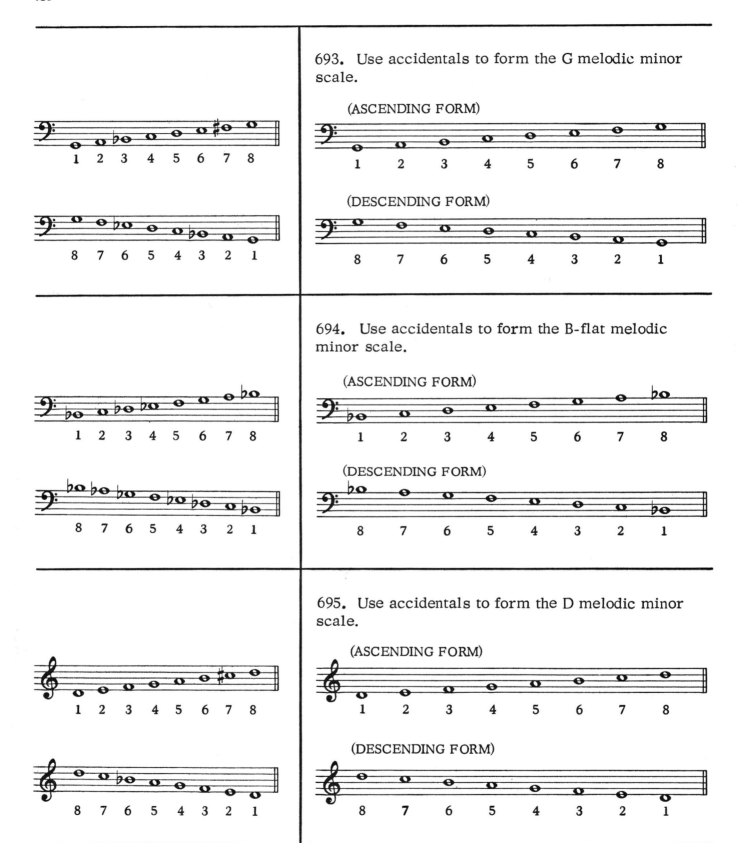

**693.** Use accidentals to form the G melodic minor scale.

(ASCENDING FORM)

1  2  3  4  5  6  7  8

(DESCENDING FORM)

8  7  6  5  4  3  2  1

**694.** Use accidentals to form the B-flat melodic minor scale.

(ASCENDING FORM)

1  2  3  4  5  6  7  8

(DESCENDING FORM)

8  7  6  5  4  3  2  1

**695.** Use accidentals to form the D melodic minor scale.

(ASCENDING FORM)

1  2  3  4  5  6  7  8

(DESCENDING FORM)

8  7  6  5  4  3  2  1

**696.** Use accidentals to form the E-flat melodic minor scale.

(ASCENDING FORM)

(DESCENDING FORM)

**697.** Use accidentals to form the A melodic minor scale.

(ASCENDING FORM)

(DESCENDING FORM)

**698.** Write the A-flat melodic minor scale.

(ASCENDING FORM)

(DESCENDING FORM)

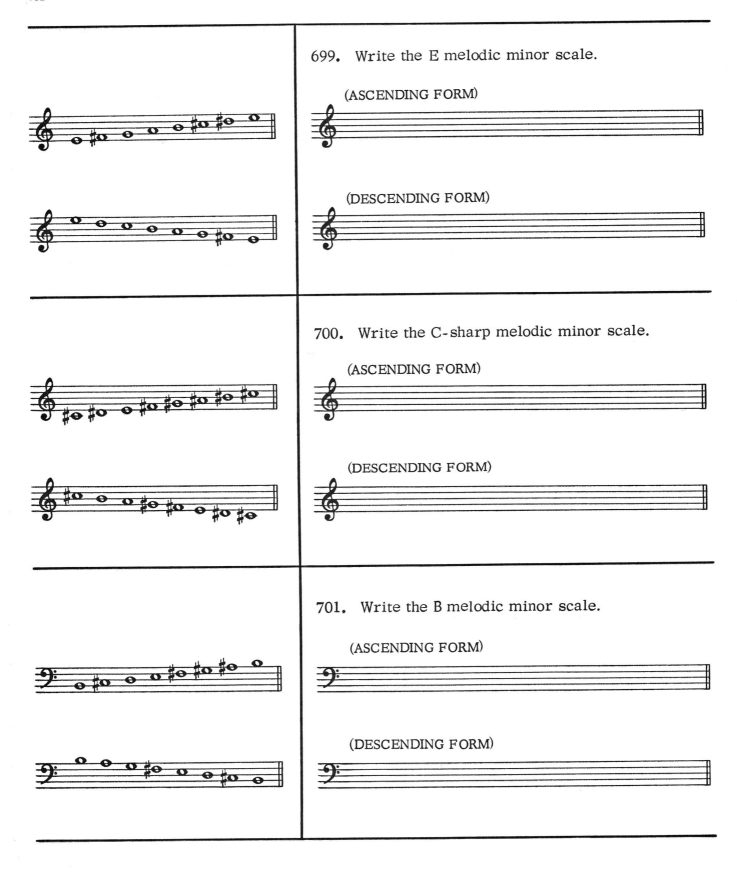

699. Write the E melodic minor scale.

(ASCENDING FORM)

(DESCENDING FORM)

700. Write the C-sharp melodic minor scale.

(ASCENDING FORM)

(DESCENDING FORM)

701. Write the B melodic minor scale.

(ASCENDING FORM)

(DESCENDING FORM)

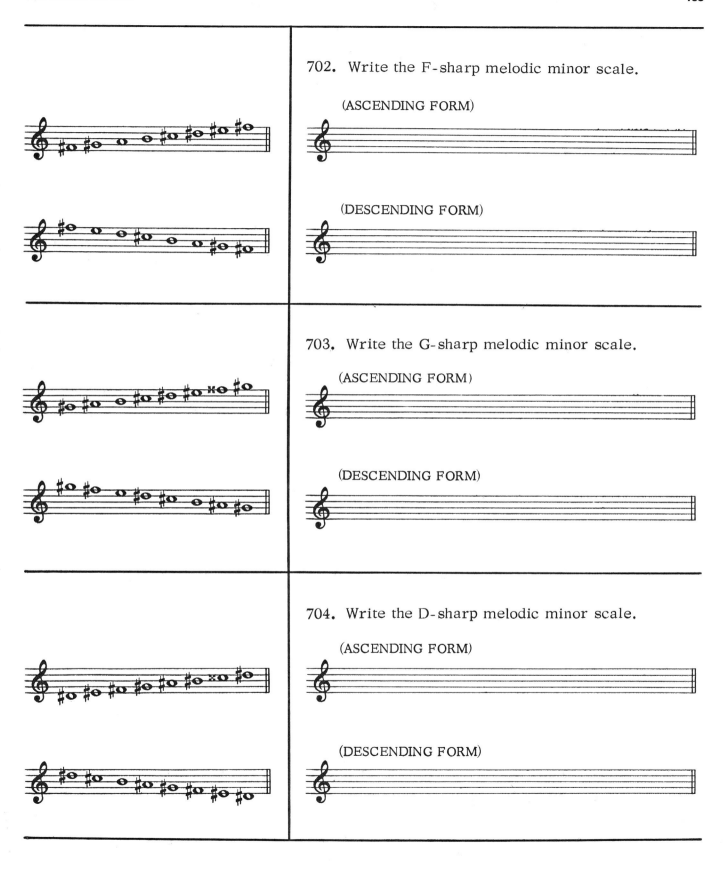

702. Write the F-sharp melodic minor scale.

(ASCENDING FORM)

(DESCENDING FORM)

703. Write the G-sharp melodic minor scale.

(ASCENDING FORM)

(DESCENDING FORM)

704. Write the D-sharp melodic minor scale.

(ASCENDING FORM)

(DESCENDING FORM)

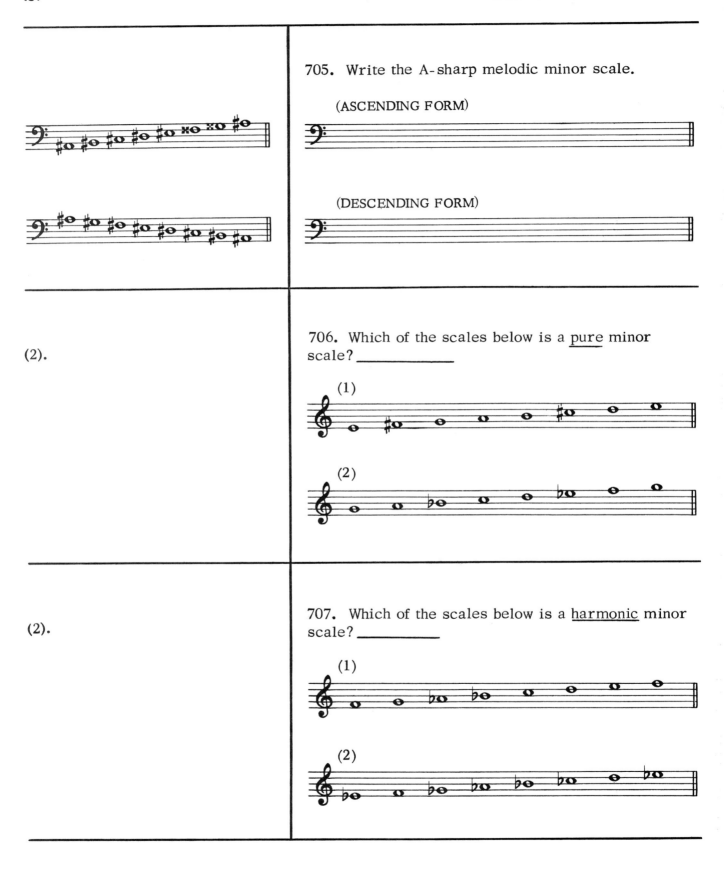

**705.** Write the A-sharp melodic minor scale.

(ASCENDING FORM)

(DESCENDING FORM)

(2).

**706.** Which of the scales below is a <u>pure</u> minor scale? _____

(1)

(2)

(2).

**707.** Which of the scales below is a <u>harmonic</u> minor scale? _____

(1)

(2)

(1).

708. Which of the scales below is the <u>ascending</u> form of a <u>melodic</u> minor scale? _____

(1)

(2)

(1).

709. Which of the scales below is the <u>descending</u> form of a <u>melodic</u> minor scale? _____

(1)

(2)

No.

710. All major and minor scales are DIATONIC scales. A diatonic scale consists of eight notes (including the octave duplication of the keynote) arranged stepwise. Does the chromatic half-step occur in any of the diatonic scales? _____

SUMMARY

The intervallic structures of the three types of minor scales are shown below:

|  | LOWER TETRACHORD | | | | UPPER TETRACHORD | | | |
|---|---|---|---|---|---|---|---|---|
| Scale degrees: | 1 | 2 | 3 | 4 | 5 | 6 | 7 | 8 |
| Natural minor: | W | H | W | W | H | W | W | |
| Harmonic minor: | W | H | W | W | H | W+H | H | |
| Melodic minor (ascending): | W | H | W | W | W | W | H | |
| Melodic minor (descending): | W | H | W | W | H | W | W | |

(W = whole-step; H = half-step)

# 10
# Key Signatures

In the preceding two chapters you learned to write major and minor scales on any note by applying various accidentals to produce the desired half- and whole-step pattern. The sharps or flats used in a particular scale may be grouped together and placed on the staff immediately after the clef sign. This is called a key signature. With a key signature it is unnecessary to apply accidentals to each altered note; for a sharp or flat in the key signature affects all such notes in any octave, unless superseded by an accidental. A knowledge of key signatures is useful in writing scales; indeed the study of scales can be based upon key signatures alone. But an appreciation for the intervallic structure of scales is best learned by first writing them without recourse to key signatures.

| | |
|---|---|
| A | 711. A scale organizes into a stepwise series of notes the tonal material of a particular KEY. The first and last note of a scale is called the KEYNOTE.<br>    The keynote of the A major scale is _____. |
| E-flat | 712. The KEY of a composition is the same as the keynote of its principal scale. If a composition is based primarily upon the E-flat major scale, it is said to be in the key of _____ major. |
| scale | 713. The term "key" is practically synonymous with TONALITY. Regardless of the term used, the keynote is the center to which the other tones of the scale relate.<br>    TONALITY is the result of causing the keynote to predominate over the remaining tones of the _____. |

| | |
|---|---|
| Tonality. | 714. Reiteration of the keynote is one way of causing it to predominate over the remaining tones of the scale; for any note which occurs more frequently than others automatically has special status. Another way is to use the keynote in strategic positions such as on metrical stresses, or at structural points such as beginnings and endings of phrases. Harmonic relationships also help establish tonality, but the study of harmony lies outside the scope of this work.<br><br>What is another word for key? _____ |
| half (and) whole | 715. Much of the music we hear today is based upon major and minor scales. Either of these can be written beginning on any note, provided the basic notes are adjusted by the use of accidentals.<br><br>Accidentals are used to produce the desired pattern of _____ - and _____ -steps. |
| sharps (or) flats | 716. The sharps or flats which are necessary to produce the desired half- and whole-step pattern in a given scale are grouped together to form the KEY SIGNATURE. The key signature is placed on the staff immediately after the clef sign, as shown below: <br><br>The key signature consists of a group of _____ or _____ . |
| B-flat | 717. The sharps or flats of a key signature apply to ALL notes of that name in the composition, unless indicated otherwise by additional accidentals.<br><br>A B-flat in the key signature means that each B appearing in the composition will be played as a _____ . |

| | |
|---|---|
| key signature | **718.** The group of sharps or flats which appear just to the right of the clef sign is called the _____ . |
| Yes. | **719.** Does a sharp or flat in the key signature affect all notes of that name regardless of where they may appear? _____ |
| F-C-G-D-A-E-B. | **720.** The sharps or flats which compose a key signature occur in a specific order. The order of the sharps is F-C-G-D-A-E-B.<br><br>Key signatures consist of either sharps or flats.* The sharps are placed on the staff in the following order:<br><br>____-____-____-____-____-____-____<br><br>*Learn the order of the sharps before proceeding with the next frame.*<br><br>*Two keys (C major and A minor) have a signature of no sharps or flats. |
| The fourth. | **721.** The sharps are placed on the staff in a particular pattern:<br><br>On which line of the treble staff does the fourth sharp appear? _____ |

The third.

**722.** In which space does the sixth sharp appear on the bass staff? _____

---

**723.** Write the seven sharps on the grand staff. *(Observe correct order and placement.)*

---

No.
*(The third sharp on the bass staff should be an octave higher.)*

**724.** Are the sharps placed correctly in the example below? _____

---

B-E-A-D-G-C-F.

**725.** The flats are placed on the staff in the following order: B-E-A-D-G-C-F. Observe that the order of the flats is the reverse of the order of the sharps. Write the order of the flats:

___-___-___-___-___-___-___

*Learn the order of the flats before proceeding with the next frame.*

**726.** The flats are placed on the staff in a particular pattern:

On which line of the treble staff does the fifth flat appear? _____

The second.

**727.** Where on the bass staff is the seventh flat placed? _____

_____

In the first space below the staff.

**728.** Write the seven flats on the grand staff. *(Observe correct order and placement.)*

**729.** Are the flats placed correctly in the example below? _____

No.
*(The last flat on both the treble and bass staff should be an octave lower.)*

730. Write once again on the grand staff the seven sharps.

731. Write once again on the grand staff the seven flats.

732. Any given key signature indicates both a MAJOR and a MINOR key. We shall learn first how to determine the MAJOR key.

    The C major scale uses only the basic (unaltered) notes. The key signature for the key of C major is therefore _____ sharps or flats.

no

733. The major key which has a signature of no sharps or flats is _____.

C major

E

734. If the key signature consists of <u>sharps</u>, the major key can be determined by referring to the LAST sharp in the signature. This sharp indicates the 7th scale degree. The keynote, therefore, is a half-step higher. (The interval of a half-step separates the 7th and 8th degrees of the major scale.)

    If the last sharp in the key signature is D-sharp, the key is _____ major.

---

The 7th.

735. Which degree of the major scale is indicated by the last sharp of the key signature? _____

---

A

736. If the last sharp in the key signature is G-sharp, the key is _____ major.

---

D

737. If the last sharp in the key signature is C-sharp, the key is _____ major.

---

B

738. What key is indicated by the signature below? _____ major.

---

G

739. What key is indicated by the signature below? _____ major.

F-sharp

740. What key is indicated by the signature below?
_____ major.

E

741. What key is indicated by the signature below?
_____ major.

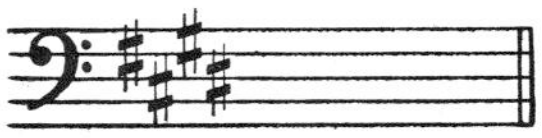

D

742. What key is indicated by the signature below?
_____ major.

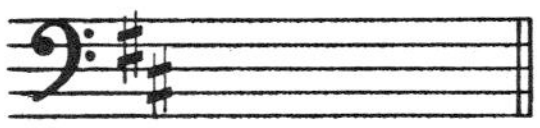

A

743. What key is indicated by the signature below?
_____ major.

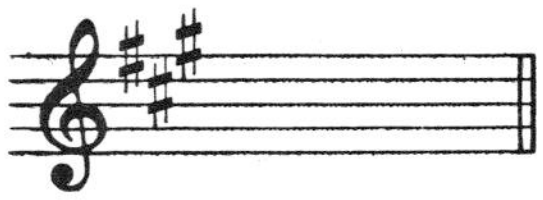

C-sharp

744. What key is indicated by the signature below?
_____ major.

**745.** To write a key signature consisting of sharps for a given key, the process described in Frame 734 is reversed. For example, the signature for the key of E major can be determined as follows:

(1)  The 7th degree of the E major scale is D-sharp.
(2)  D-sharp will be the last sharp in the key signature.
(3)  The order of sharps up to and including D-sharp is F-C-G-D.
(4)  Therefore, the signature for the key of E major is four sharps.

The last sharp of the key signature is on which degree of the major scale? _____

The 7th.

---

**746.** Write on the grand staff the key signature of A major.

---

**747.** Write on the grand staff the key signature of D major.

748. Write on the grand staff the key signature of E major.

749. Write on the grand staff the key signature of G major.

750. Write on the grand staff the key signature of B major.

**751.** Write on the grand staff the key signature of C-sharp major.

**752.** Write on the grand staff the key signature of F-sharp major.

**753.** If the key signature consists of <u>flats</u>, the major key can be determined by referring to the LAST flat in the signature. This flat indicates the <u>fourth</u> scale degree. By counting scale degrees down from the last flat (4, 3, 2, 1), the name of the key can be determined.

KEY OF A-FLAT MAJOR

4    3    2    1 (keynote)

    If the last flat of the key signature is D-flat, the key is _____ major.

A-flat

| | |
|---|---|
| The 1st. | 754. Notice in the preceding frame that the name of the key (A-flat) is the same as the next-to-the-last flat. *This will always be the case.* You may wish to make use of this method when identifying key signatures which contain flats. *<br><br>    The next-to-the-last flat indicates which degree of the major scale? _____<br><br>*The key of one flat (F major) is the only key which cannot be identified in this way. |
| D-flat | 755. If the next-to-the-last flat in the key signature is D-flat, what is the name of the key? _____ major. |
| E-flat | 756. If the next-to-the-last flat in the key signature is E-flat, what is the name of the key? _____ major. |
| D-flat | 757. What key is indicated by the signature below? _____ major.<br><br> |
| F | 758. What key is indicated by the signature below? _____ major.<br><br> |

| | |
|---|---|
| G-flat | **759.** What key is indicated by the signature below? _____ major. |
| A-flat | **760.** What key is indicated by the signature below? _____ major. |
| B-flat | **761.** What key is indicated by the signature below? _____ major. |
| E-flat | **762.** What key is indicated by the signature below? _____ major. |
| C-flat | **763.** What key is indicated by the signature below? _____ major. |

764. The signature of a key containing flats can be determined as follows:

    (1)   Go through the order of the flats until you reach the flat which is identical with the name of the key.

    (2)   Add the next flat in the series of flats.

The next-to-the-last flat is on which degree of the major scale? _____

---

The 1st.

765. The __last__ flat is on which degree of the major scale? _____

---

The 4th.

766. Write on the grand staff the key signature of E-flat major.

---

767. Write on the grand staff the key signature of B-flat major.

768. Write on the grand staff the key signature of A-flat major.

769. Write on the grand staff the key signature of F major.

770. Write on the grand staff the key signature of D-flat major.

**771.** Write on the grand staff the key signature of C-flat major.

**772.** Write on the grand staff the key signature of G-flat major.

**773.** Keys with two or more flats in their signatures have the word "flat" in their name. There are, for example, the keys of B-<u>flat</u>, E-<u>flat</u>, A-<u>flat</u>, and so forth. The key of F major (one flat) is the only "flat" key which does not have the word "flat" in its name.

The word "flat" is part of the name of all the major keys which contain flats in their signatures except the key of _____ major.

F

Sharps.

774. Would the signature for the key of E major consist of sharps or flats? _____

Flats.

775. Would the signature for the key of A-flat major consist of sharps or flats? _____

Flats.

776. Would the signature for the key of G-flat major consist of sharps or flats? _____

Sharps.

777. Would the signature for the key of B major consist of sharps or flats ? _____

778. Write on the grand staff the key signature of D major.

779. Write on the grand staff the key signature of D-flat major.

780. Write on the grand staff the key signature of G major.

781. Write on the grand staff the key signature of C major.

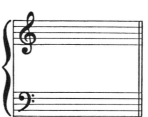

**782.** Write on the grand staff the key signature of F major.

**783.** Write on the grand staff the key signature of B major.

**784.** Write on the grand staff the key signature of B-flat major.

785. The system of major keys may be arranged in a pattern called the CIRCLE OF FIFTHS.

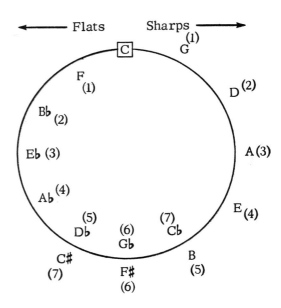

You may find the circle of fifths to be an aid in remembering the various major key signatures. Examine the order in which the sharp keys occur (reading clockwise from C major).

Each additional sharp added to the signature produces a key the interval of a _____ _____ higher than the preceding key.

perfect 5th

786. Refer again to the circle of fifths in the preceding frame. Examine the order in which the flat keys occur (reading counterclockwise from C major).

Each additional flat added to the signature produces a key the interval of a perfect 5th _____ than the preceding key.

lower

C-flat major.

787. The circle of fifths makes it clear that some of the flat keys sound the same as some of the sharp keys. The key of five flats (D-flat), for example, sounds the same as the key of seven sharps (C-sharp). Keys which contain the same pitches, but are notated differently are ENHARMONIC KEYS.

Which key is enharmonic with B major?

_____

Six sharps.
*(F-sharp major.)*

788. What is the signature of the key which is enharmonic with G-flat major? _____

major

789. Each key signature indicates not only a MAJOR key but also a MINOR key. The major and minor keys which share the same signature are called RELATIVE KEYS.

Each major key has a relative minor key, and each minor key has a relative _____ key.

3rd

790. The relation between a major key and its relative minor is shown in the example below:

White note = major keynote.
Black note = minor keynote.

The keynote of the relative minor key is located on the 6th degree of the major scale. The keynote of the relative major key is located on the _____ degree of the minor scale.

below

791. The keynotes of relative major and minor keys are a minor 3rd apart. The keynote of a minor key is a minor 3rd (above/below) _____ the keynote of its relative major.

---

relative

792. The two keys (one major and one minor) which utilize the same key signature are called _____ keys.

---

The 6th.

793. There is a relative minor key for each major key. Upon which degree of the major scale is the keynote of its relative minor located? _____

---

The 3rd.

794. There is a relative major key for each minor key. Upon which degree of the minor scale is the keynote of its relative major located? _____

---

The minor 3rd.

795. You must not think that because the keynote of the relative minor is located below the keynote of the major, or because major key signatures have been presented first, that minor keys are inferior to major keys. On the contrary, composers have long treated minor keys as in every way equal to major keys. A minor key does not borrow its signature from the relative major; a single signature is shared by the two keys.

What is the interval which separates the keynotes of relative major and minor keys?

_____

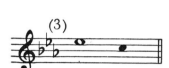

**796.** Indicate (with a black note) the keynote of the relative <u>minor</u> for each major key below:

White note = major keynote.
Black note = minor keynote.

**797.** Indicate (with a black note) the keynote of the relative <u>minor</u> for each major key below:

White note = major keynote.
Black note = minor keynote.

**798.** Indicate (with a white note) the keynote of the relative <u>major</u> for each of the minor keys below:

White note = major keynote.
Black note = minor keynote.

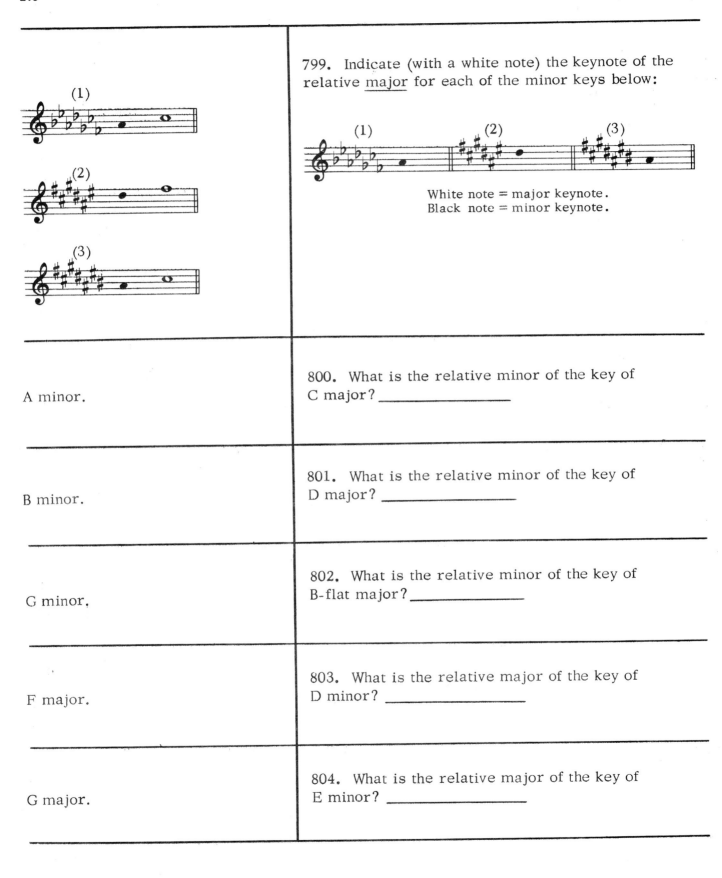

**799.** Indicate (with a white note) the keynote of the relative major for each of the minor keys below:

White note = major keynote.
Black note = minor keynote.

A minor.

**800.** What is the relative minor of the key of C major? _____

B minor.

**801.** What is the relative minor of the key of D major? _____

G minor.

**802.** What is the relative minor of the key of B-flat major? _____

F major.

**803.** What is the relative major of the key of D minor? _____

G major.

**804.** What is the relative major of the key of E minor? _____

A major.

805. What is the relative major of the key of F-sharp minor? _____

---

C minor.

806. What is the relative minor of the key of E-flat major? _____

---

807. A circle of fifths can be written for minor keys as well as major keys.

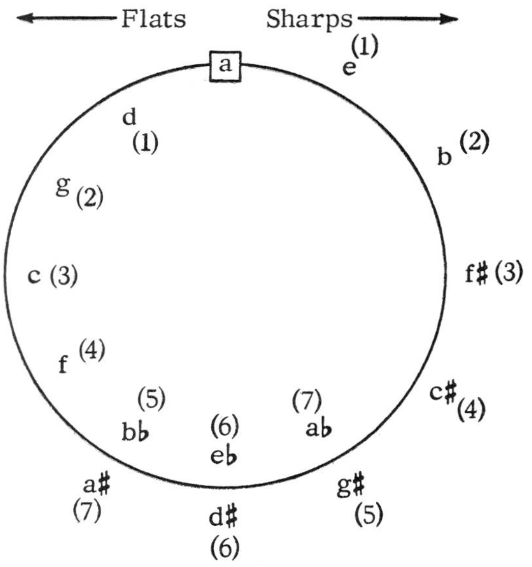

You may use the circle of fifths above as an aid in remembering minor key signatures. As in the case of major keys, each additional sharp in the signature produces a key a perfect 5th higher than the preceding key.

enharmonic

The keys of E-flat minor and D-sharp minor are _____ keys.

808. Write on the grand staff the key signature of C-sharp minor.

809. Write on the grand staff the key signature of F minor.

810. Write on the grand staff the key signature of B-flat minor.

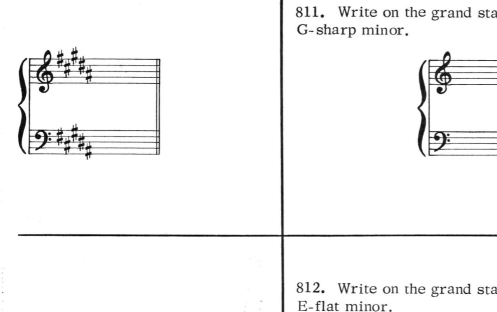

**811.** Write on the grand staff the key signature of G-sharp minor.

**812.** Write on the grand staff the key signature of E-flat minor.

**813.** Write on the grand staff the key signature of D-sharp minor.

**814.** Write on the grand staff the key signature of A-flat minor.

**815.** Write on the grand staff the key signature of A-sharp minor.

**816.** The sharps or flats of the key signature produce the half- and whole-step pattern of the NATURAL minor scale.

THE C NATURAL MINOR SCALE

1   2   3   4   5   6   7   8

What type of minor scale results when the notes are limited to the sharps or flats of the key signature? The _____ minor.

natural

817. Accidentals in addition to the sharps or flats of the key signature are necessary to transform the natural minor scale into the harmonic and melodic types. These accidentals are applied to the individual notes as needed.

THE C HARMONIC MINOR SCALE

1   2   3   4   5   6   7   8

If the 7th degree of a natural minor scale is raised a half-step, the result is the _____ minor scale.

harmonic

818. Transform the natural minor scale below into a harmonic minor scale.

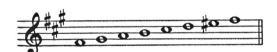

819. Transform the natural minor scale below into a harmonic minor scale.

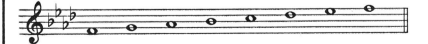

**820.** Transform the natural minor scale below into a <u>harmonic</u> minor scale.

**821.** Transform the natural minor scale below into a <u>harmonic</u> minor scale.

**822.** The <u>melodic</u> minor scale (<u>ascending</u> form) is formed by raising the 6th and 7th degrees of the natural minor scale each by a half-step.

THE C MELODIC MINOR SCALE, ASCENDING FORM

If the 6th and 7th degrees of the natural minor scale are raised each by a half-step, the result is the _____ form of the melodic minor scale.

ascending

**823.** Since the descending form of the melodic minor scale is identical with the natural minor scale, the 6th and 7th degrees must be returned to their previous state by the use of accidentals.

THE C MELODIC MINOR SCALE

The descending form of the melodic minor scale is the same as the _____ minor scale.

natural

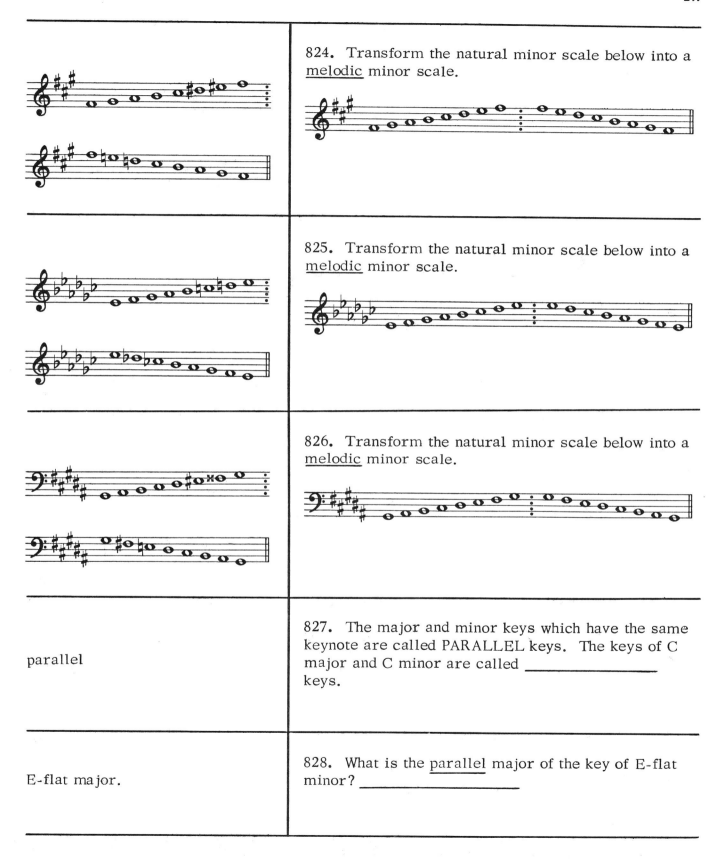

824. Transform the natural minor scale below into a <u>melodic</u> minor scale.

825. Transform the natural minor scale below into a <u>melodic</u> minor scale.

826. Transform the natural minor scale below into a <u>melodic</u> minor scale.

parallel

827. The major and minor keys which have the same keynote are called PARALLEL keys. The keys of C major and C minor are called _____ keys.

E-flat major.

828. What is the <u>parallel</u> major of the key of E-flat minor? _____

B major.

829. What is the <u>parallel</u> major of the key of B minor?

_____

E minor.

830. What is the <u>parallel</u> minor of the key of E major?

_____

F-sharp minor.

831. What is the <u>parallel</u> minor of the key of F-sharp major? _____

No.

832. PARALLEL keys have the same keynote. Do they have the same key signature?_____

No.

833. RELATIVE keys have the same key signature. Do they have the same keynote? _____

834. Use black notes to show the keynotes of the relative and parallel keys of E major.

835. Use black notes to show the keynotes of the relative and parallel keys of F minor.

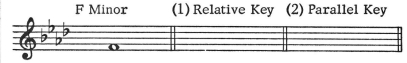

## SUMMARY

A single key signature serves for both a major and a minor key. These are called relative keys. The keynote of the relative minor is located on the sixth degree of the major scale (a minor 3rd below); the keynote of the relative major scale is located on the third degree of the minor scale (a minor 3rd above). Parallel keys have the same keynotes, but not the same signatures.

The signature of no sharps or flats denotes the keys of C major and A minor. If there are sharps in the signature, the last sharp falls on the seventh degree of the major scale; if there are flats, the last flat falls on the fourth degree of the major scale.

# 11
# Triads

The three elements of traditional music are <u>melody</u>, <u>rhythm</u>, and <u>harmony</u>. The harmonic element in most of the music we hear and play is based upon three-note chords called triads. Because of the important role harmony plays in most music, knowledge of triads and awareness of their sounds are essential for fluent reading, good intonation, and sensitive listening. Triads are written by combining various intervals, so a thorough command of interval terminology is vital. For this reason you may wish to review Chapter 6 before proceeding.

| | |
|---|---|
| three | 836. Three or more tones sounding together form a CHORD.<br>    An interval consist of two tones, but a chord consists of _____ or more tones. |
| chord | 837. Three or more tones sounding together form a _____. |
| triad | 838. The term TRIAD refers specifically to a chord of <u>three</u> tones. A chord of three tones is called a _____. |
| triad | 839. Triads are usually based on the TERTIAN system of harmony. In this system the tones of the triad are related to one another by the interval of the 3rd.<br><br>    A chord consisting of two superimposed 3rds is called a _____. |

| | |
|---|---|
| | 840. A triad may be constructed on any note of the basic scale. |
| Seven. | These triads are called BASIC TRIADS. What is the total number of basic triads? _____ |
| C E G. | 841. Spell the basic triad based on C. _____ |
| D F A. | 842. Spell the basic triad based on D. _____ |
| E G B. | 843. Spell the basic triad based on E. _____ |
| F A C. | 844. Spell the basic triad based on F. _____ |
| G B D. | 845. Spell the basic triad based on G. _____ |
| A C E. | 846. Spell the basic triad based on A. _____ |
| B D F. | 847. Spell the basic triad based on B. _____ |

No.

848. Play the seven basic triads at the piano and compare the sound of each. It is apparent they do not all sound alike. This is because the intervallic structure is not the same for all basic triads, due to the half-steps which occur between E and F, and between B and C in the basic scale.

Do the seven basic triads sound alike? _____

(1) Major
(2) Minor
(3) Diminished
(4) Augmented
*(Any order.)*

849. There are four types of triads which originate in the major-minor scale system: MAJOR, MINOR, DIMINISHED, and AUGMENTED. We shall examine each type separately.

Name the four types of triads.

(1) _____

(2) _____

(3) _____

(4) _____

major

850. The three tones of the MAJOR triad correspond to the 1st, 3rd, and 5th degrees of the <u>major</u> scale.

When sounding together, the 1st, 3rd, and 5th degrees of the major scale produce a _____ triad.

root

851. The lowest tone of a triad is called the ROOT. It is the generating tone of the triad and exerts a strong influence over the other two members (the 3rd and 5th).

The <u>lowest</u> tone of a triad (when the tones are arranged in 3rds) is called the _____.

| | |
|---|---|
| 5th | 852. The <u>uppermost</u> tone of a triad (when the tones are arranged in 3rds) is called the _____. |
| 3rd | 853. The tone between the root and 5th of a triad is called the _____. |
| 1st, 3rd, (and) 5th | 854. The MAJOR triad consists of the _____, _____, and _____ degrees of the major scale. |
| perfect 5th | 855. Observe in the example below the intervals which constitute the major triad.<br><br><br><br>In the major triad the interval from 1 up to 3 is a major 3rd, the interval from 3 up to 5 is a minor 3rd, and the interval from 1 up to 5 is a _____. |
| Minor 3rd. | 856. What is the interval from 3 up to 5 of a major triad? _____ |
| Major 3rd. | 857. What is the interval from 1 up to 3 of a major triad? _____ |

Perfect 5th.

858. What is the interval from 1 up to 5 of a major triad? _____

---

859. Three of the basic triads are major triads. These are C E G, F A C, and G B D.

Observe that the tones of each triad fall into the major scale of the root.

When sounding together, the 1st, 3rd, and 5th degrees of the major scale produce a _____ triad.

major

---

860. A major triad may be written on any note by either relating the three tones of the triad to the major scale of the root, or by observing the correct intervallic relationship between the triad tones. Try both methods; check one against the other.

Write major triads (the given note is the root).

---

861. Write major triads (the given note is the root).

862. Write major triads (the given note is the <u>root</u>).

863. Write major triads (the given note is the <u>root</u>).

864. Write major triads (the given note is the <u>root</u>).

865. Write major triads (the given note is the <u>3rd</u>).

866. Write major triads (the given note is the <u>3rd</u>).

867. Write major triads (the given note is the <u>3rd</u>).

868. Write major triads (the given note is the <u>3rd</u>).

869. Write major triads (the given note is the <u>5th</u>).

870. Write major triads (the given note is the <u>5th</u>).

871. Write major triads (the given note is the <u>5th</u>).

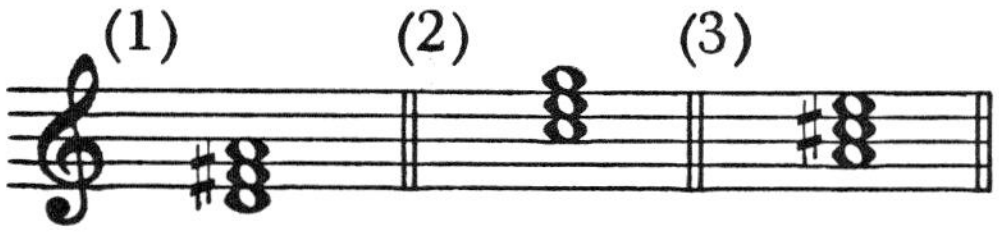

(1)    (2)    (3)

**872.** Write major triads (the given note is the <u>5th</u>).

(1)    (2)    (3)

---

C E G;  F A C;  G B D.

**873.** List the three basic triads which are <u>major</u>.

_____  _____  _____

---

**874.** A MINOR triad consists of the 1st, 3rd, and 5th degrees of the minor scale.

1  2  3  4  5  6  7  8      5 3 1

minor

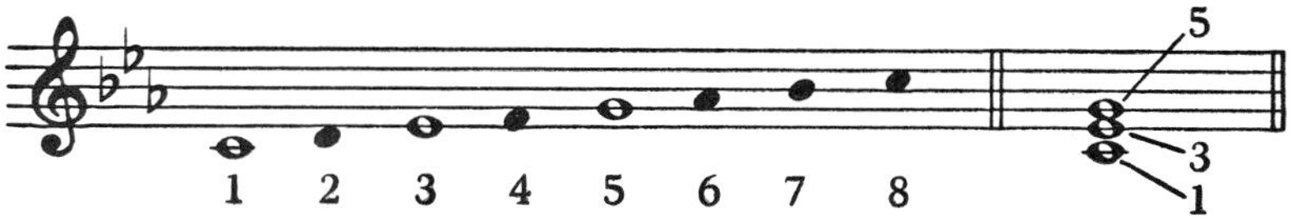

When sounding together, the 1st, 3rd, and 5th degrees of the minor scale produce a _____ triad.

---

minor

**875.** A MINOR triad consists of the 1st, 3rd, and 5th degrees of the _____ scale.

---

Minor 3rd.

**876.** The intervals which constitute the minor triad are shown below:

M3

P5    m3

What is the interval from 1 up to 3 of a minor triad? _____

Major 3rd.

877. What is the interval from 3 up to 5 of a minor triad? _____

---

Perfect 5th.

878. What is the interval from 1 up to 5 of a minor triad? _____

---

major

879. As compared with the major triad, the order of major and minor 3rds is reversed in the minor triad.

|           | MAJOR TRIAD | MINOR TRIAD |
|-----------|-------------|-------------|
| 3 up to 5 | minor 3rd   | major 3rd   |
| 1 up to 3 | major 3rd   | minor 3rd   |
| 1 up to 5 | perfect 5th | perfect 5th |

The interval from 1 up to 5 is a perfect 5th in both the major and minor triad. The interval from 3 up to 5 in the major triad is a minor 3rd; but in the minor triad the interval from 3 up to 5 is a _____ 3rd.

---

1st,
3rd, (and) 5th

880. Three of the basic triads are minor triads. These are D F A, E G B, and A C E.

The minor triad consists of the _____, _____, and _____ degrees of the minor scale.

---

881. Write minor triads (the given note is the root).

**882.** Write minor triads (the given note is the <u>root</u>).

**883.** Write minor triads (the given note is the <u>root</u>).

**884.** Write minor triads (the given note is the <u>root</u>).

**885.** Write minor triads (the given note is the <u>root</u>).

**886.** Write minor triads (the given note is the <u>3rd</u>).

887. Write minor triads (the given note is the 3rd).

888. Write minor triads (the given note is the 3rd).

889. Write minor triads (the given note is the 3rd).

890. Write minor triads (the given note is the 5th).

891. Write minor triads (the given note is the 5th).

(1) (2) (3)

892. Write minor triads (the given note is the 5th).

(1) (2) (3)

(1) (2) (3)

893. Write minor triads (the given note is the 5th).

(1) (2) (3)

(2).

894. Which of the triads below is a minor triad?____

(1) (2) (3) (4)

(3).

895. Which of the triads below is a major triad?____

(1) (2) (3) (4)

D F A; E G B; A C E.

896. List the three basic triads which are minor.

_____ _____ _____

**897.** The DIMINISHED triad can be produced by lowering the 5th of a minor triad a half-step.

If the 5th of a minor triad is lowered a half-step, the result is a _____ triad.

diminished

---

**898.** Transform the minor triads below into diminished triads by lowering the 5th a half-step.

*Apply the proper accidentals to the second triad in each case.*

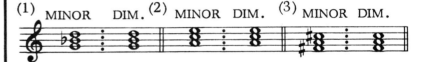

---

**899.** The DIMINISHED triad can be produced by raising the root and 3rd of a minor triad a half-step.

If the root and 3rd of a minor triad are raised a half-step, the result is a _____ triad.

diminished

**900.** Transform the minor triads below into diminished triads by raising the <u>root</u> and <u>3rd</u> a half-step.

*Apply the proper accidentals to the second triad in each case.*

(1) MINOR   DIM.  (2) MINOR   DIM.  (3) MINOR   DIM.

---

raised

**901.** The diminished triad is the same as a minor triad whose 5th has been lowered a half-step, or whose root and 3rd have been _____ a half-step.

---

Minor 3rd.

**902.** Observe the intervals which constitute the diminished triad.

The diminished triad is named for the diminished 5th between the root and the 5th of the triad. What is the interval from 3 up to 5? _____

---

Minor 3rd.

**903.** What is the interval from 1 up to 3 of a diminished triad? _____

| | |
|---|---|
| minor | **904.** The diminished triad consists of two super-imposed _____ 3rds. |
| B D F. | **905.** One of the basic triads is a diminished triad. Spell this triad. _____ |

**906.** Write diminished triads (the given note is the root).

**907.** Write diminished triads (the given note is the root).

**908.** Write diminished triads (the given note is the root).

**909.** Write diminished triads (the given note is the root).

**910.** Write diminished triads (the given note is the 3rd).

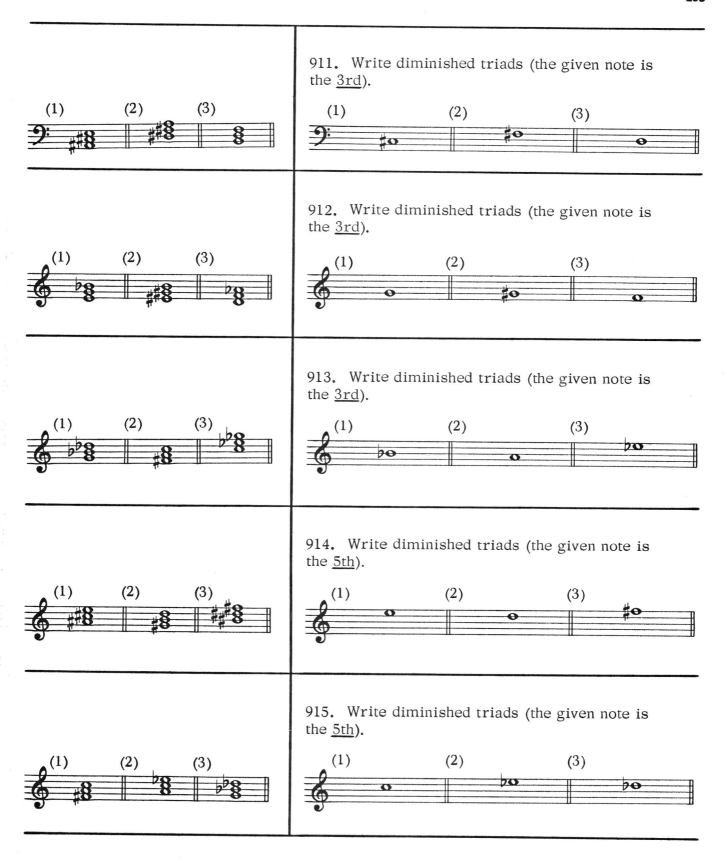

911. Write diminished triads (the given note is the 3rd).

912. Write diminished triads (the given note is the 3rd).

913. Write diminished triads (the given note is the 3rd).

914. Write diminished triads (the given note is the 5th).

915. Write diminished triads (the given note is the 5th).

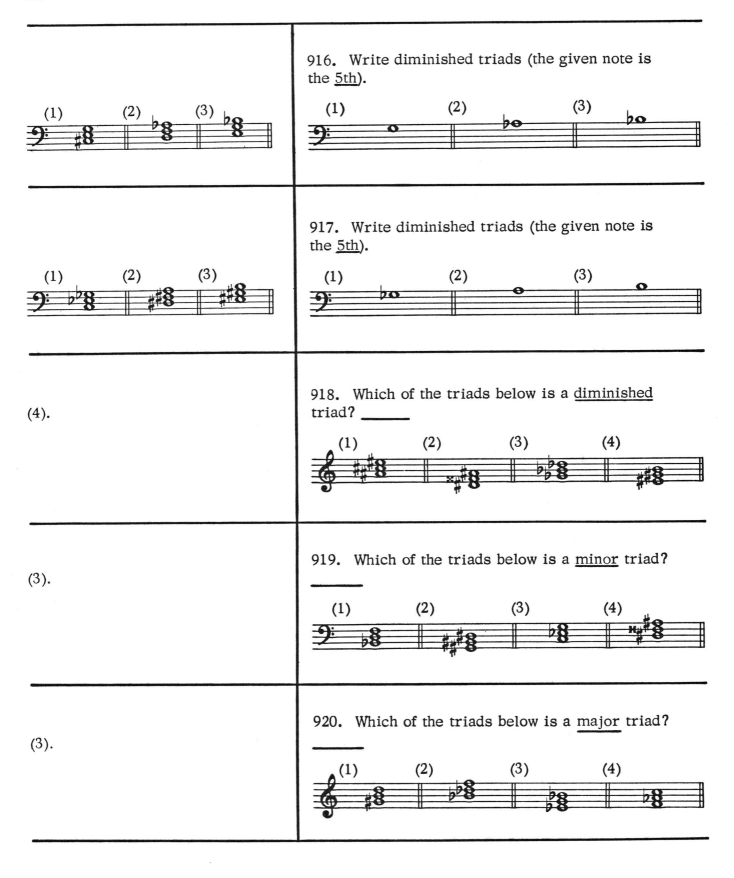

**916.** Write diminished triads (the given note is the 5th).

**917.** Write diminished triads (the given note is the 5th).

**918.** Which of the triads below is a diminished triad? _____

**919.** Which of the triads below is a minor triad?
_____

**920.** Which of the triads below is a major triad?
_____

(4).

(3).

(3).

921. The AUGMENTED triad can be produced by raising the <u>5th</u> of a major triad a half-step.

MAJOR      AUGMENTED

If the 5th of a major triad is raised a half-step, the result is a(n)_____ triad.

augmented

---

922. Transform the major triads below into augmented triads by raising the <u>5th</u> a half-step.

*Apply the proper accidentals to the second triad in each case.*

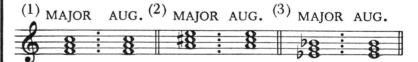

(1) MAJOR  AUG. (2) MAJOR AUG. (3) MAJOR AUG.

(1)    (2)    (3)

---

923. The AUGMENTED triad can be produced by lowering the <u>root</u> and <u>3rd</u> of a major triad a half-step.

MAJOR      AUGMENTED

If the root and 3rd of a major triad are lowered a half-step, the result is a(n) _____ triad.

augmented

**924.** Transform the major triads below into augmented triads by lowering the <u>root</u> and <u>3rd</u> a half-step.

*Apply accidentals to the second triad in each case.*

(1) MAJOR   AUG. (2) MAJOR   AUG. (3) MAJOR   AUG.

---

lowered

**925.** The augmented triad is the same as a major triad whose 5th has been raised a half-step, or whose root and 3rd have been _____ a half-step.

---

An augmented 5th.

**926.** Observe the intervals which constitute the augmented triad.

In the augmented triad the intervals from 1 up to 3, and from 3 up to 5 are both major 3rds.
What is the interval from 1 up to 5?

_____

---

major

**927.** The augmented triad consists of two super-imposed _____ 3rds.

Major; minor;
diminished.

928. The augmented triad does not exist as a basic triad. List the three types of triads which do occur as basic triads. _____

_____

929. Write augmented triads (the given note is the root).

930. Write augmented triads (the given note is the root).

931. Write augmented triads (the given note is the root).

932. Write augmented triads (the given note is the root).

**933.** Write augmented triads (the given note is the 3rd).

**934.** Write augmented triads (the given note is the 3rd).

**935.** Write augmented triads (the given note is the 3rd).

**936.** Write augmented triads (the given note is the 3rd).

**937.** Write augmented triads (the given note is the 5th).

938. Write augmented triads (the given note is the 5th).

939. Write augmented triads (the given note is the 5th).

940. Write augmented triads (the given note is the 5th).

(2).

941. Which of the triads below is an augmented triad? _____

(3).

942. Which of the triads below is a major triad? _____

(4).

943.  Which of the triads below is a <u>diminished</u> triad? _____

(3).

944.  Which of the triads below is a <u>minor</u> triad? _____

major

945.  The MAJOR triad consists of a major 3rd (1 up to 3) and a minor 3rd (3 up to 5).  The MINOR triad consists of a minor 3rd (1 up to 3) and a _____ 3rd (3 up to 5).

minor

946.  The two 3rds which constitute the major and minor triads are "unequal."  One is major and one is _____.

major

947.  The DIMINISHED triad consists of two minor 3rds (1 up to 3, and 3 up to 5).  The AUGMENTED triad consists of two _____ 3rds (1 up to 3, and 3 up to 5).

minor

948.  The diminished and augmented triads are composed of "equal" intervals.  Both of the 3rds in the diminished triad are _____ 3rds.

augmented

949. The triad which consists of two superimposed major 3rds is the _____ triad.

(1) D F♯ A.
(2) D F A.
(3) D F A♭.
(4) D F♯ A♯.

950. Spell triads as directed:
    (1) D is 1 of the major triad _____
    (2) D is 1 of the minor triad _____
    (3) D is 1 of the diminished triad _____
    (4) D is 1 of the augmented triad _____

(1) E♭ G B♭.
(2) E G B.
(3) E G B♭.
(4) E♭ G B.

951. Spell triads as directed:
    (1) G is 3 of the major triad _____
    (2) G is 3 of the minor triad _____
    (3) G is 3 of the diminished triad _____
    (4) G is 3 of the augmented triad _____

(1) F A C.
(2) F A♭ C.
(3) F♯ A C.
(4) F♭ A♭ C.

952. Spell triads as directed:
    (1) C is 5 of the major triad _____
    (2) C is 5 of the minor triad _____
    (3) C is 5 of the diminished triad _____
    (4) C is 5 of the augmented triad _____

(1) B♭ D♭ F.
(2) A♭ C E♭.
(3) F A♭ C♭.
(4) C E G♯.

953. Spell triads as directed:
    (1) B♭ is 1 of the minor triad _____
    (2) E♭ is 5 of the major triad _____
    (3) A♭ is 3 of the diminished triad _____
    (4) G♯ is 5 of the augmented triad _____

(1) C♯ E G.

(2) B♭ D F♯.

(3) D♭ F♭ A♭.

(4) C♯ E♯ G♯.

954. Spell triads as directed:

(1) G is 5 of the diminished triad _____

(2) D is 3 of the augmented triad _____

(3) A♭ is 5 of the minor triad _____

(4) C♯ is 1 of the major triad _____

## SUMMARY

Triads are chords consisting of three tones. Major and minor 3rds are used to construct triads in the tertian system. If tonal material is limited to major and minor scales, there are four types of triads: major, minor, diminished, and augmented. A major triad consists of the 1st, 3rd, and 5th tones of a major scale; a minor triad consists of the 1st, 3rd, and 5th tones of a minor scale. The diminished triad is the same as a minor triad with the 5th lowered a half-step; the augmented triad is the same as a major triad with the 5th raised a half-step.

The chart below summarizes the intervals contained in each of the triads.

| Triad | 1 up to 3 | 3 up to 5 | 1 up to 5 |
|------------|-----------|-----------|-----------|
| Major | M3 | m3 | P5 |
| Minor | m3 | M3 | P5 |
| Diminished | m3 | m3 | d5 |
| Augmented | M3 | M3 | A5 |

# Glossary of Musical Terms

*A* (It. , Fr.) - At, to, by, in, with.

*A battuta* (It.) - In strict time.

*A piacere* (It.) - At pleasure, in free time.

*A tempo* (It.) - Return to original tempo.

*A volonta* (It.) - At pleasure.

*A volonté* (Fr.) - At pleasure.

*Aber* (Ger.) - But.

*Accelerando* (It.) - Gradually growing faster.

*Ad libitum* (Lat.) - At pleasure, freely.

*Adagio* (It.) - Slowly, smoothly, gently.

*Affettuosamente* (It.) - Affectionately, tenderly.

*Affrettando* (It.) - Becoming faster, excited.

*Affrettoso* (It.) - Hurried.

*Agevole* (It.) - Light, easy, smooth, facile.

*Agitato* (It.) - Agitated, excited.

*Aimable* (Fr.) - Pleasant, agreeable.

*Aisément* (Fr.) - Easily, comfortably.

*Al* (It.) - At the, to the, on the.

*Al fine* (It.) - To the end.

*Al segno* (It.) - To the sign.

*Alla* (It.) - In the style of.

*Alla breve* (It.) - Rapid duple-simple meter in which the half note is the unit.

*Alla marcia* (It.) - In march style.

*Alla turca* (It.) - In Turkish style.

*Allargando* (It.) - Growing gradually slower.

*Allegretto* (It.) - Fast, but slower than *allegro*.

*Allegro* (It.) - Fast.

*Am* (Ger.) - On, by, near.

*Amabile* (It.) - Agreeable, tender, lovely.

*Amoroso* (It.) - Amorous.

*Ancora* (It.) - Again, yet, still, more.

*Ancora una volta* (It.) - Once more.

*Andante* (It.) - Moderately slow.

*Andantino* (It.) - Diminutive of *andante*. Usually interpreted as slightly quicker than *andante*, but may also have the opposite meaning.

*Animato* (It.) - Animated, spirited, brisk, buoyant.

*Animé* (Fr.) - Animated.

*Anmutig* (Ger.) - Graceful, charming, pleasant.

*Appassionata* (It.) - With passion.

*Aria* (It.) - Air, song.

*Arioso* (It.) - Melodious.

*Assai* (It.) - Much, very much.

*Assez* (Fr.) - Enough, quite.

*Attacca* (It.) - Join, attach, bind.

*Au* (Fr.) - To the, in the, at, for.

*Au mouvement* (Fr.) - Return to the original tempo.

*Aufhalten* (Ger.) - To retard.

*Ausdruck* (Ger.) - Expression.

*Avec* (Fr.) - With.

*Battuta* (It.) - Beat (see *A battuta*).

*Beaucoup* (Fr.) - Very, considerably.

*Behaglich* (Ger.) - Without haste, placid, comfortable.

*Bei* (Ger.) - With, at, for.

*Belebt* (Ger.) - Lively, animated.

*Ben* (It.) - Well, very.

*Beruhigend* (Ger.) - Calming.

*Bewegter* (Ger.) - Faster, more animated.

*Bien* (Fr.) - Well, very.

*Bis* (Ger.) - Until, up to.

*Bis zu Ende* (Ger.) - Until the end.

*Bravura* (It.) - Spirit, dash, skill.

*Breit* (Ger.) - Broad, stately.

*Brillante* (It.) - Sparkling, brilliant, glittering.

*Brio* (It.) - Vigor, spirit, animation.

*Brioso* (It.) - Vivacious, sprightly, animated.

*Buffa* (It.) - Comic, burlesque.

*Cadenza* (It.) - An ornamental unaccompanied passage, cadence.

*Calando* (It.) - Growing softer.

*Calore* (It.) - Warmth, ardour.

*Cantabile* (It.) - In a singing style.

*Capo* (It.) - Head, beginning.

*Capriccioso* (It.) - Whimsical, capricious.

*Cedendo* (It.) - Growing gradually slower.

*Cédez* (Fr.) - Growing gradually slower.

*Clair* (Fr.) - Light, clear, bright.

*Coda* (It.) - Literally "tail," the closing section of a composition or movement.

*Codetta* (It.) - A short *coda*.

*Col, coll, colla* (It.) - With the.

*Colla parte* (It.) - With the principal part.

*Collera* (It.) - Anger, rage.

*Come* (It.) - As, like.

*Come prima* (It.) - As before.

*Come sopra* (It.) - As above.

*Commodo* (It.) - Easy, without haste.

*Con* (It.) - With.

*Con animo* (It.) - With animation.

*Con moto* (It.) - With motion.

*Con spirito* (It.) - With spirit.

*Corto* (It.) - Short, brief.

*Coulé* (Fr.) - Smoothly.

*Crescendo (Cresc.)* (It.) - Gradually growing louder (often notated: ◁ ).

*Cuivré* (Fr.) - Play in a "brassy" way.

*Da* (It.) - From, at, by, to, for, like.

*Da, dal, dallo, dalla* (It.) - From, at, by, to, for, like.

*Da capo (D.C.)* (It.) - From the beginning.

*Dal segno (D.S.)* (It.) - From the sign.

*Dans* (Fr.) - In, within.

*Décidé* (Fr.) - Decided, resolute

*Deciso* (It.) - Decided, bold.

*Decrescendo (Decresc.)* (It.) - Gradually growing softer (often notated: ▷ ).

*Del, dell', della, delle, dello* (It.) - Of the, than the.

*Demi* (Fr.) - Half.

*Desto* (It.) - Sprightly, lively.

*Détaché* (Fr.) - Detached, short.

*Deutlich* (Ger.) - Clear, distinct.

*Di* (It.) - To, by, of, for, with.

*Di molto* (It.) - Extremely.

*Diminuendo (Dim.)* (It.) - Gradually growing softer (often notated: ▷ ).

*Dolce* (It.) - Sweet, soft, pleasant, mild, charming.

*Dolente* (It.) - Sad, painful, sorrowful.

*Dolore* (It.) - Sorrow, pain, grief, regret.

*Doppio* (It.) - Double, twice as much.

*Doppio movimento* (It.) - Twice as fast.

*Doppio più lento* (It.) - Twice as slow.

*Douce* (Fr.) - Sweet, soft, mild, calm, charming.

*Drängend* (Ger.) - Hastening, pressing ahead.

*Drückend* (Ger.) - Heavy, stressed.

*E, ed* (It.) - And.

*Edelmütig* (Ger.) - Noble, lofty.

*Eifrig* (Ger.) - Ardently.

*Eilig* (Ger.) - Hurried.

*Einfach* (Ger.) - Simple.

*En* (Fr.) - In, into, as, like, in the form of.

*En cédant* (Fr.) - Growing gradually slower.

*En dehors* (Fr.) - Outside of, to be brought out.

*En mouvement* (Fr.) - Return to original tempo.

*Espressione* (It.) - Expression, feeling.

*Espressivo* (It.) - Expressive, vivid.

*Et* (Fr.) - And.

*Etwas* (Ger.) - Somewhat.

*Facile* (It., Fr.) - Easy, simple.

*Feirlich* (Ger.) - Festive.

*Fermamente* (It.) - Firmly, resolutely.

*Fermata* (⌒) (It.) - Pause.

*Feroce* (It.) - Wild, fierce, savage.

*Festevole* (It.) - Festive, joyful, gay.

*Feu* (Fr.) - Fire, ardour, passion, spirit.

*Feuer* (Ger.) - Fire, ardour, spirit.

*Fière* (Fr.) - Proud, lofty.

*Fin* (Fr.) - End, close.

*Fine* (It.) - End, close.

*Flautando* (It.) - Flutelike, clear.

*Flüchtig* (Ger.) - Delicately, airily.
*Forte* (*f*) (It.) - Loud, strong.
*Fortissimo* (*ff*) (It.) - Very loud.
*Forzando* (It.) - With force.
*Forzato* (It.) - Forced.
*Frei* (Ger.) - Free.
*Freimütig* (Ger.) - Frankly, broad.
*Frisch* (Ger.) - Brisk, lively.
*Fröhlich* (Ger.) - Joyful, gay.
*Früheres Zeitmass* (Ger.) - The original tempo.
*Funebre* (It., Fr.) - Funereal, gloomy, dismal.
*Fuoco* (It.) - Fire.
*Furente* (It.) - Furious, frantic.
*Furioso* (It.) - Furious, violent, frantic.
*Gai* (Fr.) - Gay, cheerful, lively, pleasant.
*Gefühl* (Ger.) - Feeling, expression.
*Gehend* (Ger.) - Moderately slow (at a "walking" tempo).
*Geist* (Ger.) - Spirit.
*Gemächlich* (Ger.) - Comfortably, without haste.
*Gewichtig* (Ger.) - Ponderous, heavy.
*Giocoso* (It.) - Playful, gay, humorous.
*Giusto* (It.) - Strict, exact, precise.
*Glänzend* (Ger.) - Sparkling, brilliant.
*Gracieux* (Fr.) - Graceful, gracious.
*Grave* (It., Fr.) - Solemn, heavy, serious.
*Grazioso* (It.) - Graceful, charming, pretty.
*Heftig* (Ger.) - Impetuous, intense, furious.
*Heimlich* (Ger.) - Mysterious, stealthy.
*Heiter* (Ger.) - Serene, bright, cheerful.
*Hübsch* (Ger.) - Charming, pretty.
*Hurtig* (Ger.) - Rapid.
*I, il* (It.) - The.
*Im ersten Zeitmass* (Ger.) - In original tempo.
*Immer* (Ger.) - Always, ever.
*Immer belebter* (Ger.) - Growing more lively.
*Immer langsamer werden* (Ger.) - Growing gradually slower.
*Innig* (Ger.) - Intimate, heartfelt, ardent.
*Istesso* (It.) - Same, like.
*Istesso tempo* (It.) - The same tempo.

*Kräftig* (Ger.) - Strong, powerful.
*Lacrimoso* (It.) - Mournful, plaintive, tearful.
*Lamentoso* (It.) - Mournful, plaintive, doleful.
*Ländlich* (Ger.) - Rustic, simple.
*Langsam* (Ger.) - Slow.
*Largamente* (It.) - Broadly.
*Larghetto* (It.) - Slow, but quicker than *largo*.
*Largo* (It.) - Extremely slow, broad.
*Le même mouvement* (Fr.) - The same tempo.
*Lebhaft* (Ger.) - Lively, animated, brilliant.
*Legato* (It.) - Smooth, connected.
*Léger* (Fr.) - Light, delicate, nimble.
*Leggiero* (It.) - Light, delicate, nimble, quick.
*Leicht* (Ger.) - Light, easy.
*Leicht bewegt* (Ger.) - Light, agitated.
*Leise* (Ger.) - Soft, gentle.
*Lent* (Fr.) - Slow.
*Lento* (It.) - Slow.
*Lesto* (It.) - Quick, nimble, lively.
*Licenza* (It.) - Freedom, license.
*Lieblich* (Ger.) - Charming, sweet.
*L'istesso tempo* (It.) - The same tempo.
*Lontano* (It.) - Distant, soft.
*Lungo* (It.) - Long.
*Lustig* (Ger.) - Playful, merry.
*Ma* (It.) - But, however.
*Ma non troppo* (It.) - But not too much.
*Mächtig* (Ger.) - Powerful.
*Maestoso* (It.) - Majestic, stately, grand.
*Mais* (Fr.) - But.
*Mais pas trop* (Fr.) - But not too much.
*Mal* (Ger.) - Time, occurrence.
*Mancando* (It.) - Decreasing, dying away.
*Marcato* (It.) - Marked, accentuated, pronounced.
*Marcia* (It.) - March.
*Marcia funebre* (It.) - Funeral march.
*Marziale* (It.) - Martial, warlike.
*Mässig* (Ger.) - Moderate, the equivalent of *andante*.

*Mässig bewegt* (Ger.) - With moderate animation.

*Mehr* (Ger.) - More.

*Même* (Fr.) - Same.

*Même mouvement* (Fr.) - The same tempo.

*Meno* (It.) - Less.

*Mesto* (It.) - Sad, mournful, gloomy.

*Mezzo* (It.) - Half, middle.

*Mezzo forte* (*mf*) (It.) - Moderately loud.

*Mezzo piano* (*mp*) (It.) - Moderately soft.

*Misura* (It.) - Measure.

*Mit* (Ger.) - With.

*Moderato* (It.) - At a moderate tempo.

*Modéré* (Fr.) - Moderate, reasonable.

*Möglich* (Ger.) - Possible.

*Möglichst* (Ger.) - As much as possible.

*Moins* (Fr.) - Less.

*Molto* (It.) - Very, greatly, well.

*Morendo* (It.) - Dying away.

*Mosso* (It.) - Rapid, animated.

*Moto* (It.) - Motion, movement.

*Munter* (Ger.) - Lively, vigorous, the equivalent of *allegro*.

*Nicht* (Ger.) - Not.

*Nicht zu schnell* (Ger.) - Not too fast.

*Nicht zu viel* (Ger.) - Not too much.

*Nieder* (Ger.) - Low.

*Niente* (It.) - Nothing.

*Noch* (Ger.) - Yet, still.

*Noch einmal* (Ger.) - Once more.

*Non* (It.) - Not, no.

*Non troppo* (It.) - Not too much.

*Nur* (Ger.) - Only, merely.

*Oder* (Ger.) - Or, or else.

*Ohne* (Ger.) - Without.

*Opus* (Lat.) - Work.

*Oscuro* (It.) - Dark, dim, mysterious.

*Ossia* (It.) - Or, or rather.

*Ou* (Fr.) - Or.

*Parlando* (It.) - In a speaking manner

*Pas* (1) (Fr.) - Step, pace, dance.

*Pas* (2) (Fr.) - Not, no.

*Pas beaucoup* (Fr.) - Not too much.

*Pas du tout* (Fr.) - In nowise.

*Pausa* (It.) - Pause, rest.

*Perdendosi* (It.) - Dying away.

*Pesante* (It.) - Heavy, ponderous.

*Peu* (Fr.) - Little, not much, not very.

*Peu à peu* (Fr.)' Little by little, gradually.

*Piacere* (It.) - Pleasure, delight (see *A piacere*).

*Piacevole* (It.) - Agreeable.

*Pianissimo* (*pp*) (It.) - Very soft.

*Piano* (*p*) (It.) - Soft, quiet.

*Pietoso* (It.) - Doleful, pitiful, plaintive.

*Più* (It.) - More.

*Più mosso* (It.) - Faster.

*Più moto* (It.) - More motion, faster.

*Placabile* (It.) - Placid, mild.

*Plötzlich* (Ger.) - Sudden, abrupt.

*Plus* (Fr.) - More.

*Po* (It.) - Little.

*Pochissimo* (It.) - Very little.

*Poco* (It.) - Little.

*Poco a poco* (It.) - Little by little.

*Poi* (It.) - Then, afterwards.

*Portamento* (It.) - Connected, very legato.

*Portato* (It.) - Sustained, lengthened.

*Precipitato* (It.) - Sudden, hurried.

*Pressé* (Fr.) - Hurried, in haste.

*Pressez* (Fr.) - Hurry, press ahead.

*Prestissimo* (It.) - Extremely fast.

*Presto* (It.) - Very fast.

*Prima* (It.) - First.

*Prima volta* (It.) - The first time.

*Quasi* (It.) - Almost, as if, nearly.

*Rallentando* (It.) - Gradually becoming slower.

*Rasch* (Ger.) - Rapid, lively.

*Rattenendo* (It.) - Becoming slower.

*Rattenuto* (It.) - Held back.

*Recitativo* (It.) - A speechlike passage.

*Retenir* (Fr.) - To hold back, to moderate.

*Risoluto* (It.) - Resolute, energetic, determined.

*Ritardando* (*rit.*, *ritard.*) (It.) - Gradually becoming slower.

*Rubato* (It.) - Robbed, irregular time.

*Ruhig* (Ger.) - Quiet, tranquil.

*Sans* (Fr.) - Without, free from.

*Scherzando* (It.) - Joking, playful.

*Scherzo* (It.) - Joke, jest.

*Schnell* (Ger.) - Rapid, equivalent of *presto*.

*Schwer* (Ger.) - Heavy, ponderous.

*Secco* (It.) - Dry, hard, short.

*Segno* (It.) - The sign.

*Segue* (It.) - Follows.

*Sehr* (Ger.) - Very, much, greatly.

*Semplice* (It.) - Simple, easy, unpretentious.

*Semplicemente* (It.) - Simply, plainly.

*Sempre* (It.) - Always, ever.

*Senza* (It.) - Without, free from.

*Sforzando* (*sf* or *sfz*) (It.) - A sudden, strong accent.

*Sforzata* (It.) - Forced.

*Simile* (It.) - Similar, in the same manner.

*Sin' al fine* (It.) - Until the end.

*Sin' al segno* (It.) - Until the sign.

*Singend* (Ger.) - In a singing style.

*Slancio* (It.) - With dash, boldly.

*Smorzando* (It.) - Extinguishing the sound, growing softer.

*Sostenuto* (It.) - Sustained.

*Sotto* (It.) - Under, below.

*Sotto voce* (It.) - In a low, soft voice.

*Später* (Ger.) - Later, after.

*Spirito* (It.) - Spirit.

*Spiritoso* (It.) - Spirited, vivacious, jocular.

*Staccato* (It.) - Detached, short.

*Stark* (Ger.) - Strong, heavy, loud.

*Streng* (Ger.) - Strict.

*Stretto* (It.) - Pressed, hurried.

*Stringendo* (It.) - Hastening, accelerating.

*Stürmisch* (Ger.) - Stormy, impetuous.

*Subito* (It.) - Sudden, quick, at once.

*Tacet* (It.) - To be silent.

*Takt* (Ger.) - Measure, beat, tempo.

*Takthalten* (Ger.) - In strict time.

*Tanto* (It.) - So much, as much (*Non tanto* - Not too much).

*Tempo* (It.) - Time, movement, rate of speed.

*Tempo primo* (It.) - The original tempo.

*Tenir* (Fr.) - To hold.

*Tenuto* (It.) - Sustained, held.

*Toujours* (Fr.) - Always, ever.

*Tranquillo* (It.) - Tranquil, quiet, peaceful, calm.

*Traurig* (Ger.) - Sad, pensive.

*Très* (Fr.) - Very, greatly.

*Triste* (It., Fr.) - Sorrowful, mournful, sad.

*Trop* (Fr.) - Too, too much.

*Troppo* (It.) - Too, too much (*Non troppo* Not too much).

*Tutti* (It.) - All, whole.

*Übermütig* (Ger.) - Gay, playful.

*Un, una, uno* (It.) - One.

*Un, une* (Fr.) - One.

*Un peu* (Fr.) - A little.

*Ungefähr* (Ger.) - Approximate.

*Unruhig* (Ger.) - Restless, agitated.

*Va* (It.) - Continue.

*Veloce* (It.) - Rapid, quick, nimble.

*Vif* (Fr.) - Brisk, lively, animated.

*Vigoroso* (It.) - Vigorous, robust.

*Vivace* (It.) - Lively, vivacious.

*Vivo* (It.) - Lively, brisk, animated.

*Voce* (It.) - Voice.

*Voix* (Fr.) - Voice, tone, sound.

*Volante* (It.) - With delicate, rapid execution.

*Volta* (It.) - Time, occurrence.

*Wehmütig* (Ger.) - Doleful.

*Wenig* (Ger.) - Little.

*Weniger* (Ger.) - Less.

*Wie* (Ger.) - As, like.

*Wütend* (Ger.) - Furious.

*Zart* (Ger.) - Tender, soft, delicate.

*Zeitmass* (Ger.) - Tempo, time.

*Ziemlich* (Ger.) - Moderately.

*Zögernd* (Ger.) - Growing gradually slower.

*Zurückhalten* (Ger.) - Hold back.

# Supplementary Assignments

## ASSIGNMENT 1

Chapter 1. *The Basic Materials of Music: Time and Sound*

1. Rhythm is concerned with the basic material of music called _____.
2. Pitch is a property of the basic material of music called _____.
3. Name several vibrating bodies which are capable of generating sound.
   _____
4. What transmits sound from a vibrating body to the ear? _____
   _____
5. Which property of sound is concerned with the "highness" or "lowness" of a sound? _____
   _____
6. Which frequency would produce the "higher" tone? _____
   a. 620 vibrations per second.
   b. 310 vibrations per second.
7. A tone whose frequency is double that of another sounds an _____ higher.
8. The "loudness" or "softness" of a sound is known as _____.
9. Amplitude is a term which refers to the amount of energy transmitted by the _____
   _____.
10. The technical term which refers to tone quality is _____.
11. Write the natural harmonic series through the eighth partial on each of the given notes.

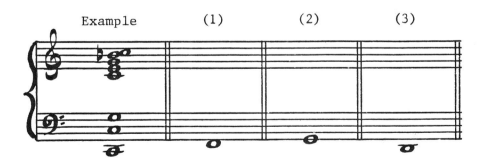

12. Name the four properties of sound.

   1. _____    2. _____

   3. _____    4. _____

13. Select the item on the right which corresponds most closely to each term on the left. (*Write the appropriate number.*)

   1.  Intensity          _____        1.  The note A
   2.  Pitch              _____        2.  First partial
   3.  Overtone           _____        3.  Time
   4.  Duration           _____        4.  Loudness/softness
   5.  Tone quality       _____        5.  Source of sound
   6.  Vibrating body     _____        6.  Timbre
   7.  Sound wave         _____        7.  2:1 frequency ratio
   8.  Octave             _____        8.  Third partial
   9.  Frequency = 440    _____        9.  Transmitter of sound
   10. Fundamental        _____        10. Frequency

NAME: _____

ASSIGNMENT 2

Chapter 2.  *The Notation of Pitch*

1.  Indicate how the lines and spaces of the staff are numbered.

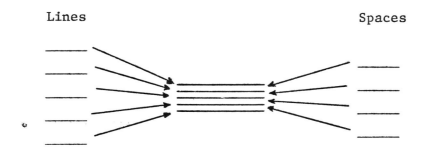

Lines                                                    Spaces

2.  Name each of the clef signs.

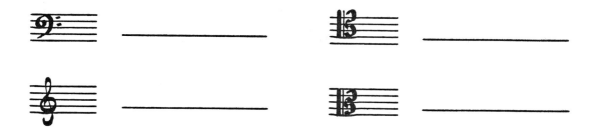

3.  Complete the information.

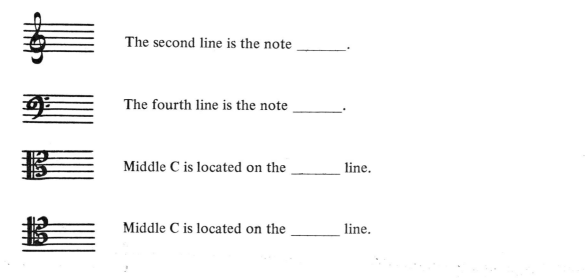

The second line is the note _____.

The fourth line is the note _____.

Middle C is located on the _____ line.

Middle C is located on the _____ line.

4. Music for the piano is usually notated on the _____ staff.
5. Write "middle C" as directed.

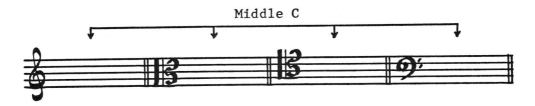

6. Name each note.

7. Indicate that the notes are to sound as directed.

8. Use the sign ∧ to show where half-steps occur.

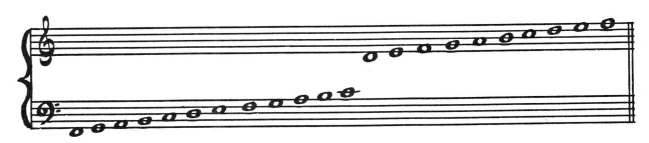

NAME: _____

## ASSIGNMENT 3

Chapter 2.  *The Notation of Pitch*

1.  What is meant by the term "basic note"? _____
    _____

2.  Write the accidental which:

    1.  raises a basic note a half-step          _____
    2.  raises a basic note a whole-step         _____
    3.  lowers a basic note a half-step          _____
    4.  lowers a basic note a whole-step         _____
    5.  cancels a previous accidental            _____

3.  Write an enharmonic equivalent for each note.

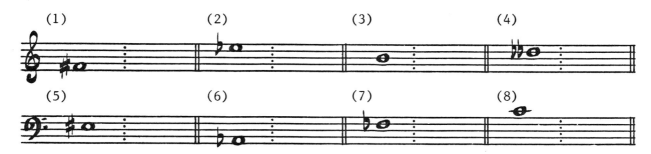

4.  List (by number) the *chromatic* half-steps. _____

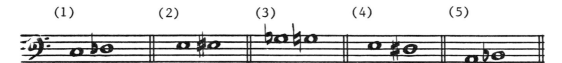

5.  List (by number) the *diatonic* half-steps. _____

6. Write a chromatic scale from middle C to the C an octave higher.

7. Write notes as directed. (*Use the* ottava *sign to avoid excessive ledger lines.*)

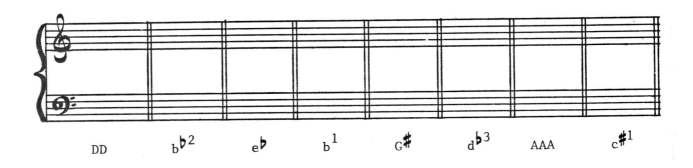

DD      b♭2      e♭      b1      G#      d♭3      AAA      c#1

NAME: _____

ASSIGNMENT 4

Chapter 3.  *Time Classification*

1.  The impulses which divide time into equal durations for musical purposes are called _____ _____ .

2.  To what does the term "meter" refer? _____
    _____

3.  The stress pattern ⟩ ᴗ ⟩ ᴗ is called _____ meter.

4.  Indicate the stress pattern for triple meter. _____

5.  Quadruple meter has _____ beats per measure.

6.  Explain how quadruple meter differs from two measures of duple meter.
    _____
    _____
    _____

7.  Write two different examples which show stress patterns in quintuple meter. (Use the symbols ⟩ and ᴗ .)

    a.  _____
    b.  _____

8.  Consistent division of beats into two equal parts is called _____ time.

9.  Consistent division of beats into three equal parts is called _____ time.

10. The term triple-simple means there are _____ beats per measure, and beats are normally divided into _____ equal parts.

11. The term duple-compound means there are _____ beats per measure, and beats are normally divided into _____ equal parts.

12. If there are four beats per measure and beats are normally divided into three equal parts, the time classification is _____ - _____ .

13. If there are five beats per measure and beats are normally divided into two equal parts, the time classification is _____ - _____ .

14. "Triplets" are borrowed divisions in _____ time.

15. Borrowed divisions in compound time are called _____ .

16.  The normal subdivision of the beat in simple time is into _____ equal parts.

17.  The normal subdivision of the beat in compound time is into _____ equal parts

NAME: _____

ASSIGNMENT 5

Chapter 4. *Note and Rest Values*

1. Indicate the names for the various symbols below:

2. On the line supplied, write an example of the notes indicated.

```
Half        Quarter  Whole    32nd      Eighth    16th
```

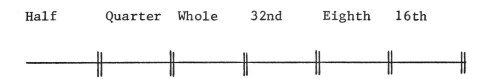

3. Supply the information required.

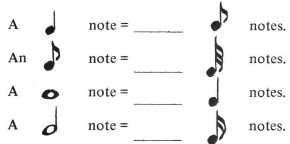

A ♩ note = _____ ♪ notes.

An ♪ note = _____ notes.

A 𝅝 note = _____ notes.

A ♩ note = _____ notes.

4. On the line supplied, write an example of each of the rests indicated.

```
Quarter   32nd     Half     16th      Whole     Eighth
```

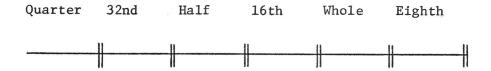

5. Supply the information required.

_____   𝄾 rests = 1 ▬ rest.

_____   ▬ rests = 4 𝄽 rests.

_____   𝄾 rests = 1 𝄽 rest.

_____   𝄾 rests = 2 𝄾 rests.

6. Explain the function of a single dot added to a note or rest. _____

_____

_____

Show with tied notes the value of each dotted or doubly-dotted note.

𝅗𝅥. = _____

𝅘𝅥.. = _____

𝅘𝅥𝅮... = _____

𝅘𝅥𝅯. = _____

NAME: _____

ASSIGNMENT 6

Chapter 4.  *Note and Rest Values*

1.  Show the division and subdivision of each unit.

| Unit | Division | Subdivision |
|------|----------|-------------|

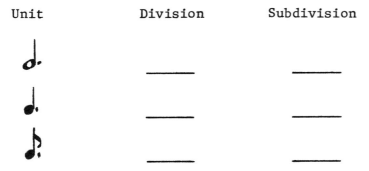

2.  Show the division and subdivision of each unit.

| Unit | Division | Subdivision |
|------|----------|-------------|

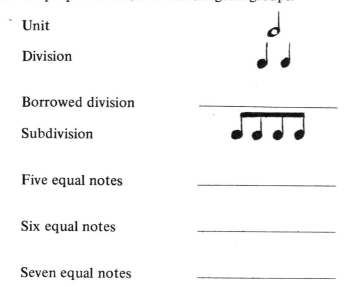

3.  Undotted notes *divide* normally into _____ equal parts: dotted notes *subdivide* normally into _____ parts.

4.  Show the proper notation for the irregular groups.

Unit

Division

Borrowed division    _____

Subdivision

Five equal notes     _____

Six equal notes      _____

Seven equal notes    _____

5. Show the proper notation for the irregular groups.

Unit

Borrowed division _____

Division

Four equal notes _____

Five equal notes _____

Subdivision

Seven equal notes _____

6. Write three notes which can serve as the unit in each case.

SIMPLE TIME        COMPOUND TIME

_____        _____

7. Supply the information required.

*Number per*
*Minute*

_____

( ♩ = 120 ) { ♩ ; ♪ ; ♫ }

_____

_____

_____

( ♪. = 120 ) { ♩. ; ♪ ; ♬ }

_____

_____

NAME: _____

ASSIGNMENT 7

Chapter 5. *Time Signatures*

1. Indicate whether each time signature represents simple or compound time.

| | SIMPLE | COMPOUND | | SIMPLE | COMPOUND |
|---|---|---|---|---|---|
| 3<br>4 | _____ | _____ | 15<br>16 | _____ | _____ |
| 6<br>8 | _____ | _____ | 9<br>4 | _____ | _____ |
| 5<br>4 | _____ | _____ | 3<br>2 | _____ | _____ |
| 7<br>8 | _____ | _____ | 4<br>8 | _____ | _____ |
| 12<br>8 | _____ | _____ | 2<br>4 | _____ | _____ |

2. The upper number of a *simple* time signature indicates _____ ;
the lower number indicates _____ .

3. To determine the number of beats per measure indicated by a *compound* time signature, the
upper number must be divided by _____ .

4. Explain how the unit may be deduced from the lower number of a *compound* time
signature. _____
_____

5. Give the proper name for each time signature below:

      a. ¢ _____

      b. C _____

6. Supply information about each time signature.

| (1) | (2) | (3) | (4) | (5) | (6) |
|-----|-----|-----|-----|-----|-----|
| 12  | 2   | 5   | 9   | 6   | C   |
| 16  | 2   | 4   | 8   | 4   |     |

|       | Beats Per Measure | Unit |
|-------|:-----------------:|:----:|
| (1)   | _____            | ____ |
| (2)   | _____            | ____ |
| (3)   | _____            | ____ |
| (4)   | _____            | ____ |
| (5)   | _____            | ____ |
| (6)   | _____            | ____ |

NAME: _____

## ASSIGNMENT 8

Chapter 5. *Time Signatures*

1. Rewrite the rhythm using beams in such a way that the meter is clearly expressed.

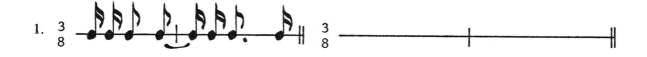

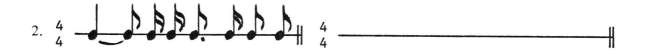

2. What is meant by the term "syncopation?" _____

_____

_____

3. Alter the rhythm by the use of ties to provide an example of syncopation.

4.  Provide the correct time signature for each measure.

ASSIGNMENT 9

Chapter 6. *Intervals*

1.  List the four intervals in group 1 (those which use the terms perfect, diminished, and augmented).

    (1) ＿＿＿＿＿    (2) ＿＿＿＿＿    (3) ＿＿＿＿＿    (4) ＿＿＿＿

2.  List the four intervals in group 2 (those which use the terms major and minor, but not perfect).

    (1) ＿＿＿＿    (2) ＿＿＿＿    (3) ＿＿＿＿    (4) ＿＿＿＿

3.  Analyze each interval.

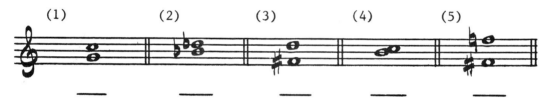

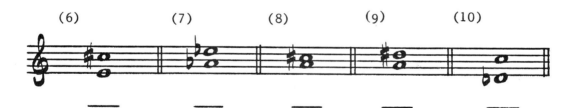

4.  Complete the information.

    When inverted at the octave:

    Minor intervals become ＿＿＿＿＿＿＿＿＿ .

    Major intervals become ＿＿＿＿＿＿＿＿ .

    Diminished intervals become ＿＿＿＿＿＿＿＿＿ .

    Augmented intervals become ＿＿＿＿＿＿＿＿ .

    Perfect intervals become ＿＿＿＿＿＿＿＿ .

5. Complete the information.

When inverted at the octave:

Unisons become _____ .

Seconds become _____ .

Thirds become _____ .

Fourths become _____ .

Fifths become _____ .

Sixths become _____ .

Sevenths become _____ .

Octaves become _____ .

6. Invert each interval, and analyze both the original and inverted interval.

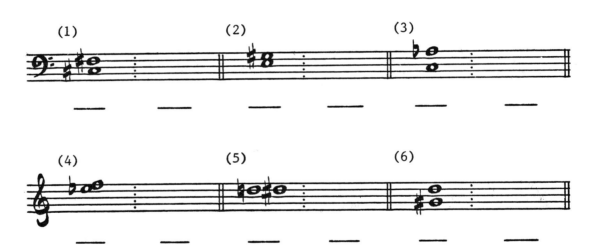

NAME _____

ASSIGNMENT 10

Chapter 6. *Intervals*

1. Write notes to produce the indicated intervals *above* the given notes.

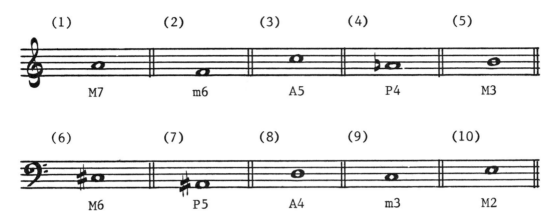

2. Write notes to produce the indicated intervals *below* the given notes.

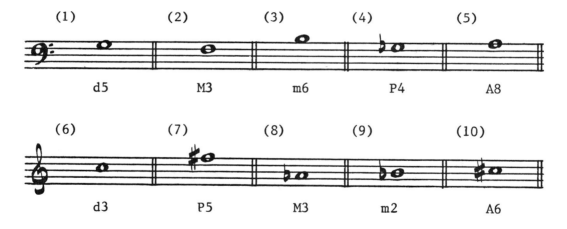

3. The intervals below have been so drastically altered that the terms major, minor, diminished, and augmented do not suffice. Provide the proper analysis of each interval. (*You may refer to Frames 533-535.*)

4.  With reference to the intervals in the preceding question:

The enharmonic equivalent of (1) is a (n) ———————— .

The enharmonic equivalent of (2) is a (n) ———————— .

The enharmonic equivalent of (3) is a (n) ———————— .

The enharmonic equivalent of (4) is a (n) ———————— .

The enharmonic equivalent of (5) is a (n) ———————— .

5.  Complete the information.

1.  All basic 2nds are ———————— except E- F and B- C, which are ———————— .

2.  All basic 3rds are ———————— except C- E, F- A, and G- B, which are ———————— .

3.  All basic 4ths are ———————— except F- B, which is ———————— .

4.  All basic 5ths are perfect except ————, which is diminished.

5.  All basic 6ths are major except ————, ————, and ————, which are minor.

6.  All basic 7ths are minor except ————, and ————, which are major.

NAME: ————————————————————

## ASSIGNMENT 11

Chapter 7. *Basic Scales*

1. Write a basic scale beginning on each note. Show with the sign ∧ where half-steps occur in each scale.

2. Explain why, although the same notes occur in each basic scale, no two sound alike. _____ .

_____

_____

3. The first and last notes of a scale are called the _____ .

4. All basic scales are diatonic scales. (True/False) _____

5. Complete the information below:

MODE:                          BASIC SCALE ON THE NOTE:

Lydian        =                    _____

Ionian        =                    _____

Dorian        =                    _____

Mixolydian    =                    _____

Locrian       =                    _____

Aeolian       =                    _____

Phrygian      =                    _____

NAME: _____

ASSIGNMENT 12

Chapter 8. *The Major Scale*

1. The major scale consists of only whole- and half-steps. There is a whole-step between successive scale degrees except between _____ – _____ , and _____ – _____ .

2. The lower and upper tetrachords of the major scale contain the same sequence of intervals. Indicate these intervals. (*Use the abbreviations: W = whole-step; H = half-step.*)

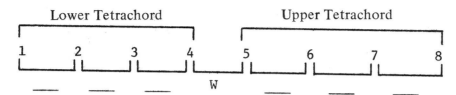

3. Which is a major scale? _____

4. Which is a major scale? _____

5. Write a major scale on each note.

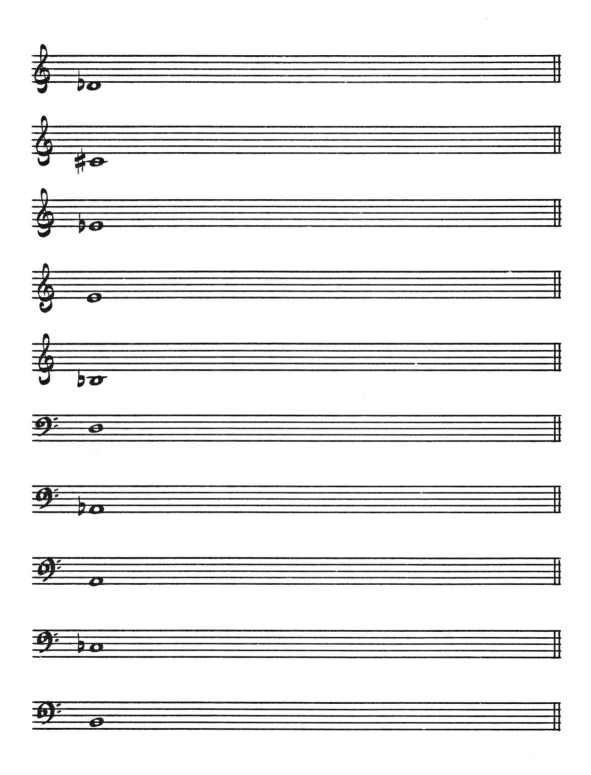

NAME: _____

ASSIGNMENT 13

Chapter 9.  *The Minor Scales*

1.  The natural minor scale is the same as the _____ mode.

2.  Between which scale degrees do half-steps occur in the natural minor scale? _____

3.  Add accidentals to form natural minor scales.

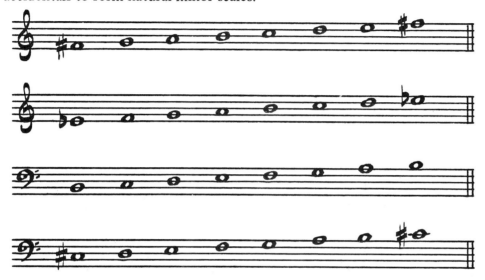

4.  Between which scale degrees do half-steps occur in the harmonic minor scale? _____

5.  What interval occurs between the 6th and 7th degrees of the harmonic minor scale? _____

6.  Add accidentals to form harmonic minor scales.

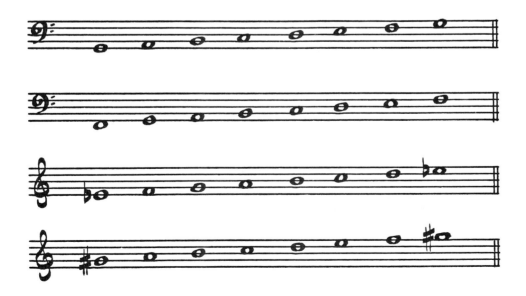

7.  Between which scale degrees do half-steps occur in the *ascending* form of the melodic minor scale? _____

8.  Between which scale degrees do half-steps occur in the *descending* form of the melodic minor scale? _____

9.  Add accidentals to form melodic minor scales.

ASSIGNMENT 14

Chapter 10. *Key Signatures*

1.  Indicate the order in which sharps and flats are placed on the staff to form key signatures.

    Sharps: _____ - _____ - _____ - _____ - _____ - _____ - _____

    Flats:  _____ - _____ - _____ - _____ - _____ - _____

2.  Write the sharps and flats on the grand staff. (*Observe correct order and placement.*)

    Sharps

    Flats

3.  What major key is indicated by a signature of no sharps or flats? _____

4.  Explain how the major key is determined if the signature consists of sharps. _____
    _____
    _____

5.  Explain how the major key is determined if the signature consists of flats. _____
    _____
    _____

6.  Each major key has a relative minor key which uses the same signature. The minor key is located a minor 3rd (above/below) _____ the major key.

7. Supply the information required.

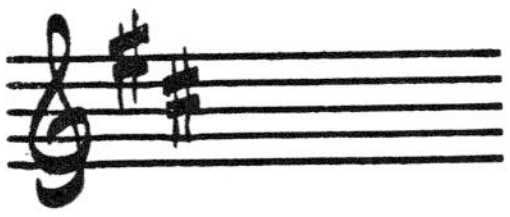

Major key: _____

Minor key: _____

Major key: _____

Minor key: _____

Major key: _____

Minor key: _____

Major key: _____

Minor key: _____

Major key: _____

Minor key: _____

Major key: _____

Minor key: _____

NAME: _____

ASSIGNMENT 15

Chapter 10.  *Key Signatures*

1. Write key signatures on the grand staff as directed. (*Capital letter = major; lower case letter = minor.*)

2. The minor scale below uses only the notes supplied by the key signature. It is a _____ minor scale.

e:

3. Transform the scale below into a *harmonic* minor scale by applying the necessary accidentals.

e:

4. Transform the scale below into a *melodic* minor scale by applying the necessary accidentals.

c:

5. The signature below indicates the key of F-sharp major. Supply the additional information required.

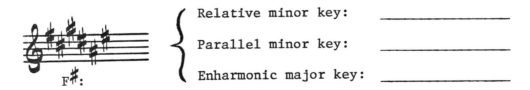

F♯:

{
    Relative minor key:     _____

    Parallel minor key:     _____

    Enharmonic major key:     _____
}

6. The signature below indicates the key of A-flat minor. Supply the additional information required.

a♭:

{
    Relative major key:     _____

    Parallel major key:     _____

    Enharmonic minor key:     _____
}

NAME: _____

## ASSIGNMENT 16

Chapter 11.  *Triads*

1.  Indicate the quality of the basic triads. (*Use the abbreviations M, m, d, and A.*)

2.  Analyze the intervals which constitute the four types of triads.

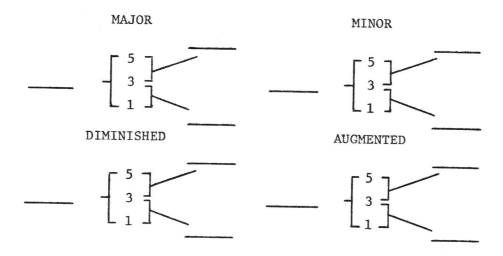

3.  Write *major* triads as indicated.

4. Write *minor* triads as indicated.

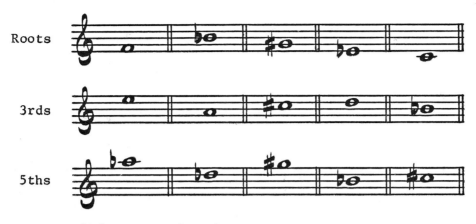

5. Write *diminished* triads as indicated.

6. Write *augmented* triads as indicated.

NAME: _____

# Eartraining Tips

Full musical comprehension requires both the ear and the mind; sounds and their related symbols must be *sensed* as well as *understood*. An extensive eartraining program is usually needed to develop aural discrimination. These eartraining tips, however, have a more modest objective: to reinforce your understanding of the material presented in this text. The exercises are suggestive rather than comprehensive. In most cases, they do not provide sufficient drill for developing aural mastery. They should, however, be a useful supplement to class experiences. They may also serve as models for further self-help.

Musicians must become acutely sensitive to sounds and time relations. For you to develop sensitivity, more than just passive listening is required. You must analyze both the sounds and the way those sounds affect you. By being aware of your response to musical stimuli, you will enlarge your mastery of musical expression.

This book is designed to help you acquire musical knowledge largely on your own. These eartraining tips are provided to help achieve this goal. The exercises may be used by you alone or along with another person, each checking the other. Some exercises may seem simple, even naive. But they serve an important function: to encourage keen, critical, and analytical listening.

Chapter 1.  *The Basic Materials of Music: Time and Sound*

1.  Tap, or strike with a pencil, any object which happens to be near you. Listen for differences in effect; analyze your responses to these simple stimuli. Are the sounds soothing/stimulating, hard/soft, high/low, short/long?

2.  Notice the effect sounds that are near by or far away have on you.

3.  Pluck a stretched rubber band. Listen to variations of pitch and observe how the rubber band vibrates as the tension is varied.

4.  At the piano play notes that are within your vocal range and match their pitches with your voice.

5.  Play notes outside your vocal range and match them within your vocal range.

6.  Sing octave intervals, both up and down. (Check yourself at the piano.)

7.  Sing the tones of the natural harmonic series on various pitches. Bring the tones within your vocal range as in the following:

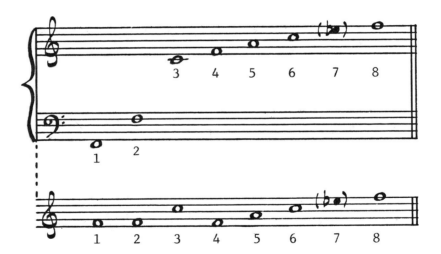

Chapter 2.  *The Notation of Pitch*

1.  Notes written on the staff in alphabetical sequence (A–G) produce a series of half- or whole-
    steps. It is essential that you recognize the difference between these two intervals. The staff
    produces two half-steps, and five whole-steps. The clef sign determines where the half-steps occur.
       Sing the notes below using each of the clefs indicated in turn. (Check pitches at the piano.)

2.  Sing the following exercises noting the differences between half- and whole-steps.

(Sing with <u>la</u>)

       The above exercises may be sung on any pitch provided the half- and whole-step relation-
    ships are the same.

3.  Sing chromatic intervals as in the following:

4.  Sing, whistle, or "think" half- and whole-steps in various patterns of your own invention.

Chapter 3.   *Time Classification*

Musicians must develop a keen sense of time passing and the various ways time is organized for musical purposes. There are three basic levels of rhythmic organization: (1) the beat; (2) meter; and (3) the division and subdivision of the beat.

The rhythm of most traditional music is based on beats of equal duration; the ability to maintain a steady beat is fundamental to effective performance. Perhaps the best and most accessible resource available to help you develop a feeling for a steady beat is the naturally regular gait of normal walking. Walking also serves as an ideal background for thinking or humming rhythmic patterns.

1.   While walking (or marking time) form a mental image that suggests steady movement of a point through space. Then imagine that your steps mark off segments of the line created by the moving point. Create your own image, but the mental association of time and space is useful within many musical contexts, tonal as well as rhythmic.

2.   Experience the various meters by thinking, clapping, or humming accents as in the following:

   a. duple meter       >   ⌣   >   ⌣

   b. triple meter      >   ⌣   ⌣   >   ⌣   ⌣

   c. quadruple meter   >   ⌣   >   ⌣   >   ⌣   >   ⌣

   d. quintuple meter   >   ⌣   ⌣   >   ⌣   or   >   ⌣   >   ⌣   ⌣

3.   By thinking, saying "ta," clapping, or by any other means, divide beats into two or three equal parts to produce simple or compound time as in the following:

   a. duple simple

      beats       >        ⌣        >        ⌣

      divisions   ⊢ — ⊦ — ⊢ — ⊦ —

   b. duple compound

      beats       >        ⌣        >        ⌣

      divisions   ⊢ — — ⊦ — — ⊢ — — ⊦ — —

4.   Sing songs such as those in Frames 201 and 202 in the main text, focusing your attention on the rhythmic structure.

Chapter 4. *Note and Rest Values*;      Chapter 5. *Time Signatures*

Music, the most abstract of all the arts, is often difficult to approach in a concrete way. Sometimes, mental imagery or analogy can assist us in comprehending and effectively interpreting a musical figure or phrase. This is true, not only of subtle nuances of phrasing, but also of basics such as note values and rhythmic patterns. The notation of music itself causes us to think in this way. Graphically, the time (rhythmic) element of music is represented on a horizontal plane; the sound (pitch) element is represented on a vertical plane.

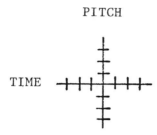

The ability to form musical images mentally varies. Even though few of us are endowed with photographic memories for images we have seen, less literal images can also be helpful. Thus, you should devise your own mental associations and form images which help you.

Visualize as vividly as you can what music notation looks like. Because printed notes are spaced approximately proportionate to their duration, mental pictures of rhythmic patterns can help you to perform figures properly.

1.  The basic rhythmic patterns which occur in *simple time* are notated as follows:

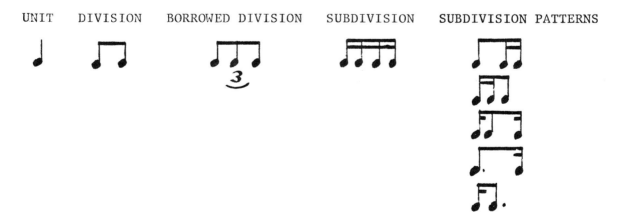

Against a steady beat (supplied by walking, or by a metronome), practice each of these patterns separately and in combinations of your own invention. Imagine (write out, if necessary) the patterns with the eighth note and the half note as the unit.

It is within the context of these simple exercises that your ability to make mental associations will grow. Do not neglect this type of drill.

2.  Apply the methods described in number 1 to the following rhythmic patterns which occur in *compound time*.

UNIT     DIVISION     BORROWED DIVISION     SUBDIVISION     **SUBDIVISION PATTERNS**

Chapter 6. *Intervals*

1. The numerical classification of intervals stems from the number of basic notes encompassed by the interval. The following exercise will help you to associate numbers with interval size.

    You may begin on any pitch, but the higher notes must be included in the major scale of the lowest note. (Major scales are presented in Chapter 8.)

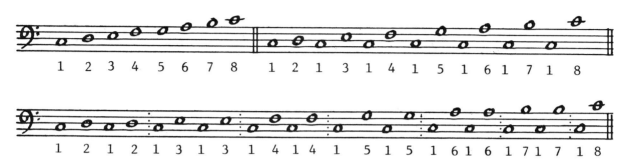

1 2 3 4 5 6 7 8   1 2 1 3 1 4 1 5 1 6 1 7 1 8

1 2 1 2 1 3 1 3 1 4 1 4 1 5 1 5 1 6 1 6 1 7 1 7 1 8

2. In the preceding exercise the intervals are sung upward from the stationary note C. The direction is reversed in the following exercise:

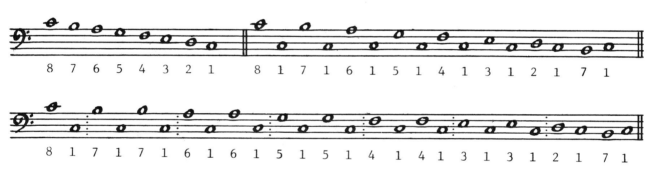

8 7 6 5 4 3 2 1   8 1 7 1 6 1 5 1 4 1 3 1 2 1 7 1

8 1 7 1 7 1 6 1 6 1 5 1 5 1 4 1 4 1 3 1 3 1 2 1 7 1

3. *Perfect Intervals (Unison, 4th, 5th, Octave).* The perfect unison and the perfect octave are perhaps the easiest of all intervals to hear. The two notes of the unison have the same pitch and in the case of the octave, one note is virtually the replica of the other. Nevertheless, when notes lie outside our own vocal ranges, it is sometimes difficult to duplicate them by ear. It is desirable, therefore, that you practice matching pitches both within and outside your range. Play widely spaced notes at the piano in order that each will be disassociated with the preceding note.

    The following example may serve as a model. Sing after each note.

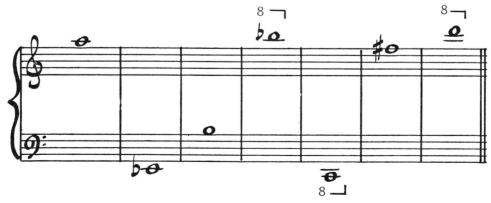

The numbers associated with the intervals in the next exercise reflect the numerical classification (5th, 4th). Play the first note at the piano; then sing the second two notes. (Check your responses, if necessary.)

4. *Augmented 4th, Diminished 5th (Tritones).* The tritone is easy to recognize, but sometimes difficult to sing. The peculiar effect of this interval stems from the facts that three whole tones are encompassed, and that the interval divides the octave into two equal parts. The augmented 4th and the diminished 5th are enharmonic. It is useful, however, to approach them as related to perfect 4ths and 5ths. Sing the following exercises:

Fifths

Diminished 5ths

5. *Major and Minor 2nds.*

($O$ = play; $\bullet$ = sing)

6. *Major and Minor 7ths.*   The octave can be helpful in learning to sing 7ths. This will be shown in the exercises that follow. (Sing with numbers if they help, otherwise use *la.*)

7. *Major and Minor 3rds.*

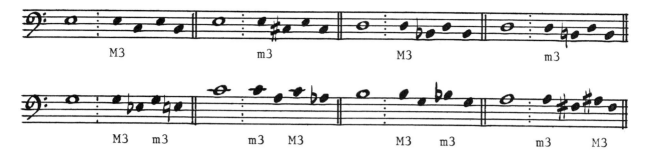

8. *Major and Minor 6ths.* The first few exercises show the relationships of major and minor 3rds to their inversions (minor and major 6ths respectively).

Major 6ths

Minor 6ths

Chapter 7.  *The Basic Scales*

By associating the numbers 1–8 with the various scale degrees, a feeling for tonal relations and for the key note is developed. Letter names or a syllable such a *la* may also be used.

Sing the various basic scales. Be alert to the half- and whole-steps. (Half-steps are indicated by the sign ⋀ .)

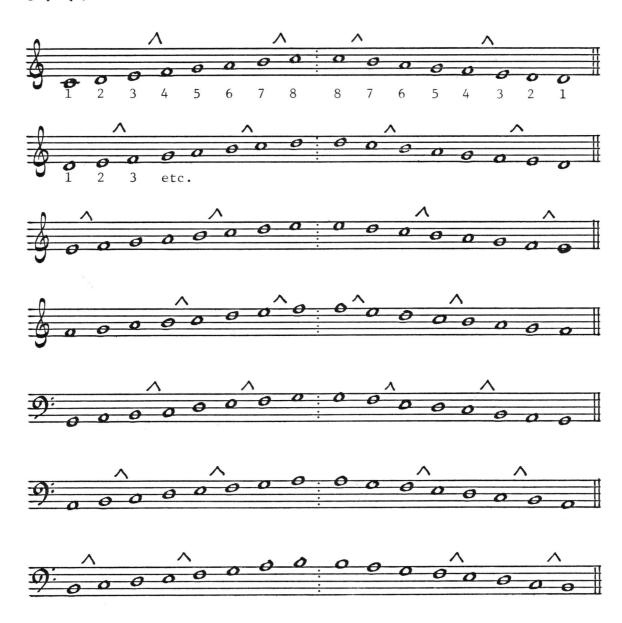

Chapter 8.  *The Major Scale*

1.  Sing the following scales. Be alert to the half-steps which occur between 3–4 and 7–8.

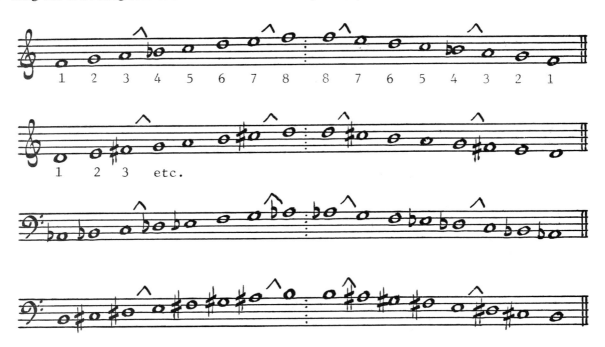

2.  Use the note A as the 1st, 2nd, 3rd, and 4th degrees of a major scale as indicated in the following exercise. Try to do this exercise by ear. Use your knowledge of the half- and whole-step pattern of the major scale. Resort to the piano for aid, if necessary.

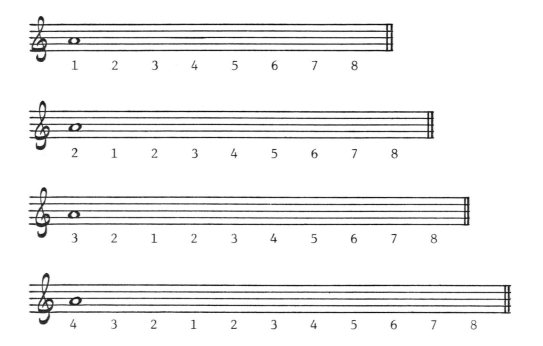

3. Use the note C as the 5th, 6th, 7th, and 8th degrees of a major scale as indicated in the following exercise. Proceed as in the last exercise.

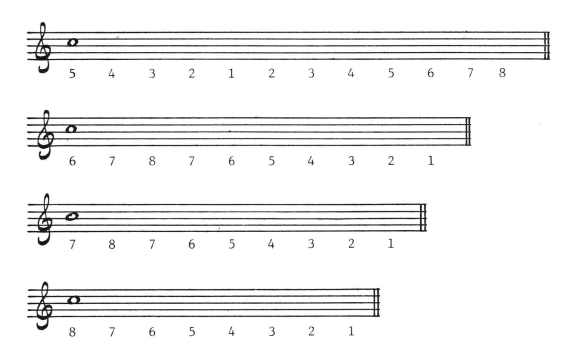

Chapter 9. *The Minor Scales*

1. The *lower* tetrachord (scale degrees 1-4) of all three forms of the minor scale is the same. The interval pattern is whole-step/half-step/whole-step. Sing the following tetrachords:

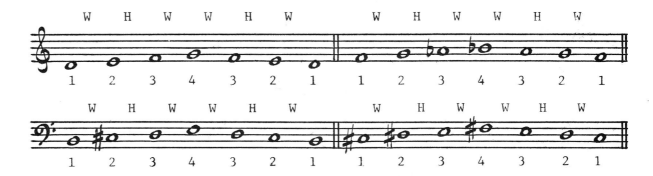

2. Focus your attention on the *upper* tetrachord as you sing the following three minor scales:

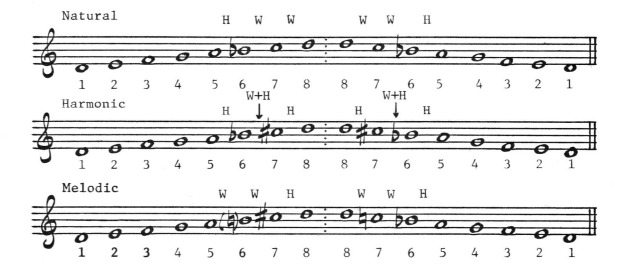

3. Practice singing the three forms of the minor scale beginning on various notes to achieve accuracy and fluency. Always be conscious of the half- and whole-step pattern. Check yourself at the piano, if necessary.

4. Use the notes given in the following to sing the various minor scales as directed. Rely on your ear and your knowledge of the intervallic pattern of each scale. Resort to the piano for aid, if necessary. End by writing out the notes of the scale.

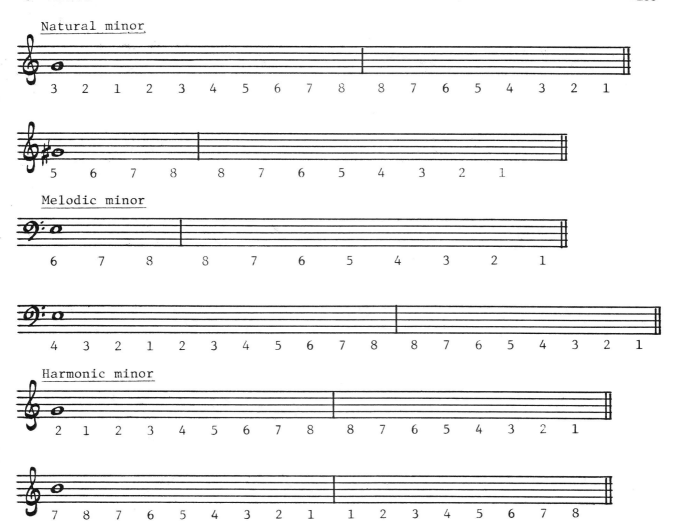

Chapter 10.  *Key Signatures*

1.  The circle of fifths (Frames 785 and 807 in the main text) is helpful in remembering the various key signatures. It is also helpful for understanding harmonic relations such as chord progressions and modulations, topics of more advanced theory study. If you begin on the lowest C of the piano, you may play the entire series of fifths in ascending motion.

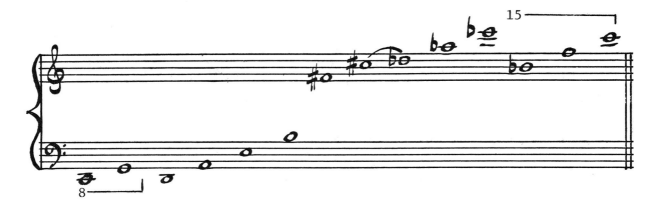

2.  The series can be sung within your vocal range by bringing all the notes within a limited range. Sing the circle of fifths as notated in the following (or transpose to a more convenient level):

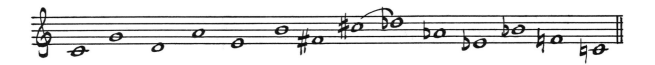

Chapter 11.  *Triads*

1.  Play the seven basic triads at the piano, taking note of the effect of each type.

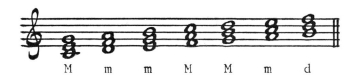

2.  Sing the basic triads according to the following model:

3.  Sing *major* triads as indicated by the following:

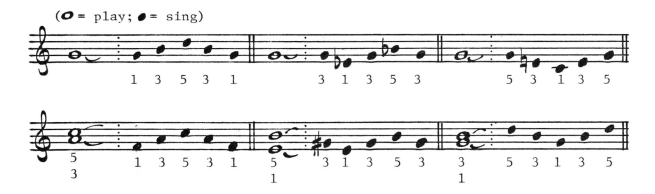

4.  Sing *minor* triads as indicated by the following:

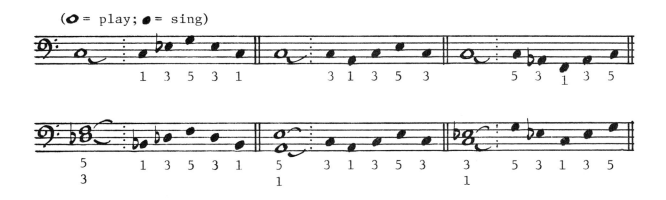

5.  Sing *diminished* triads as indicated by the following:

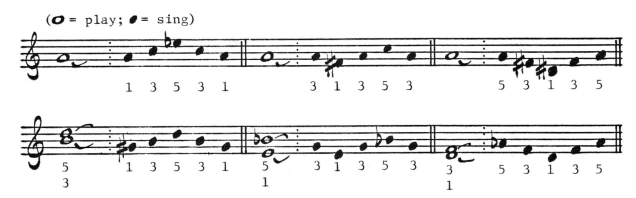

6.  Sing *augmented* triads as indicated by the following:

# Index

*(Numbers refer to frames.)*

Accidentals, 114, 116-130, 442-443, 555, 715
    affect on notes in other octaves, 130
    placement, 116
    verbal expressions, 124
Acoustics, 27, 430
Aeolian minor scale (*see* Scales, natural minor)
Aeolian mode, 554, 556, 569
*Alla breve*, 388
Alphabetical sequence of notes, 53, 98, 100, 108
Alto clef, 63-66
Amplitude, 19-20
Ascending form of melodic minor scale, 673-676, 683-684, 687
Augmented intervals (*see* Intervals, augmented)
Augmented second, 644-645, 661
Augmented triad (*see* Triads, augmented)

Bar line, 125-127
Basic fifths, 469
Basic fourths, 462
Basic notes, 114-116, 431, 546-547, 555
Basic scale (*see* Scales, basic)
Basic seconds, 495
Basic thirds, 504
Basic triads (*see* Triads, basic)
Bass clef, 55-60, 78
Beam, 265-268, 415-421
Beat, 162-250
    division, 191-236
    subdivision, 191, 237-240

Borrowed division, 230-236, 247-248
Brace, 78
Breve, 251

C-clef, 62-70
C major scale, 581-583, 732-733
Chord, 836-839 (*see also* Triads)
Chromatic half-step, 140-141, 143, 710
Chromatic scale (*see* Scales, chromatic)
Chromatic succession of notes, 139
Church modes, 554
Circle of fifths:
    major keys, 785-787
    minor keys, 807
Clefs, 51-70
Common time, 387
Compound intervals (*see* Intervals, compound)
Compound time, 192, 194, 196, 198, 200, 202-206, 232, 238, 240-241, 244, 246, 248, 250, 317, 338-339, 370
    division of the unit, 355-361
Compression, 3
Contra octave, 158-161

Descending form of melodic minor scale, 673, 677-682
Diatonic, 539 (*see also* Stepwise)
Diatonic half-step, 140-142
Diatonic scale (*see* Scales, diatonic)
Diatonic succession of notes (*see* Stepwise succession of notes)
Diminished intervals (*see* Intervals, diminished)
Diminished triad (*see* Triads, diminished)
Division of beats (*see* Beat, division)

*Dodekachordon*, 554
Dorian mode, 554, 560, 563, 573
Dot, 288-295, 297, 305, 308
Double-flat, 116, 119
Double-sharp, 116-117, 129
Double whole note, 251
Double whole rest, 278
Duple-compound (*see* Time classification, duple-compound)
Duple meter (*see* Meter, duple)
Duple-simple (*see* Time classification, duple-simple)
Duplet, 232, 250 (*see also* Borrowed division)
Duration, 40-45

Ear, 2-4, 19, 25-26
Eighth note, 251-252, 256
Eighth rest, 278, 281
Enharmonic intervals (*see* Intervals, enharmonic)
Enharmonic keys, 787-788, 807
Enharmonic notes, 132-138

F-clef (*see* Bass clef)
Fifth (*see* Intervals, fifth)
Flag, 252, 256-259, 265-266
Flat, 116, 118, 122
   use in chromatic scale, 144-145
Foreign groups (*see* Irregular groups)
Four-line octave, 149, 161
Fourth (*see* Intervals, fourth)
Frequency, 5-16, 28, 30
Fundamental, 28-33, 35

G-clef (*see* Treble clef)
Glareanus, 554
Grand staff, 78-79
Great octave, 154-156, 161

Half note, 251
Half rest, 278-279
Half-step, 96-100, 134, 139-143, 495, 547-548
Harmonic interval (*see* Intervals, harmonic)

Harmonic minor scale (*see* Scales, harmonic minor)
Harmonics, 27 (*see also* Partials)
Harmony, 34
Head (*see* Note head)

Intensity, 17-26, 45
Intervals, 96, 98
   augmented, 445, 448-451, 454-457, 462-465, 485, 489, 491, 515, 529, 532
   compound, 434-436
   definition, 427
   diminished, 445, 451, 454-455, 457, 469-470, 485, 489, 491, 515
   doubly-augmented, 533-535
   doubly-diminished, 533-535
   enharmonic, 528-535
   fifth, 443, 469-475
   fourth, 443, 462-468
   Group I, 443, 445-488
   Group II, 443, 489-527
   harmonic, 427-428
   inversion, 476-488, 514-520, 525
   major, 489-491, 495-500, 504, 515
   melodic, 427-428
   minor, 489-491, 495-497, 504, 515
   numerical classification, 430-442
   octave, 433, 436, 443, 452-459
   perfect, 445-447, 451-457, 462-465, 469-470, 485
   second, 433, 443, 489, 491, 495-503, 514
   seventh, 433, 443, 489, 491, 514, 519-520
   simple, 435
   sixth, 433, 443, 489, 491, 494, 514, 518
   third, 433, 442-443, 489, 491, 493, 504-514
   unison, 433, 443-451
Inversion (*see* Intervals, inversion)
Ionian mode, 554-555, 558, 568, 571, 584
Irregular groups, 308-312

Key, 711-714
Key-center (*see* Keynote)

Key signatures, 716-835
Key signatures:
   major keys, 732-785
   minor keys, 789-815
   order of flats, 725-729
   order of sharps, 720-724
Keynote, 573-580, 590, 710-711, 713-714,
   790-799

Ledger lines, 71-77
   limitation, 86
   spacing, 71
Leger lines (*see* Ledger lines)
Lines, 46-47, 50-51
   numbering, 50
Locrian mode, 554, 562, 566
Loudness (*see* Intensity)
Lower tetrachord (*see* Tetrachords)
Lydian mode, 554, 559, 567, 570, 608

Mälzel Metronome, 331
Major intervals (*see* Intervals, major)
Major scale (*see* Scales, major)
Major triad (*see* Triads, major)
Major-minor scale system, 849
Major-minor tonal system, 554
Measure, 125-126, 128-129, 189-190
Melodic minor scale (*see* Scales, melodic
   minor)
Meter, 164-190, 313-315, 353
   duple, 167-168, 171-173, 196-198,
      201-202, 205-206
   duple-compound, 359
   duple-simple, 388
   quadruple, 173-176, 196
   quadruple-simple, 387
   quintuple, 178-183, 196
   triple, 169-173, 196
   triple-compound, 374
   triple-simple, 373
Metrical organization, 339
Metronome (*see* Mälzel Metronome)
Mezzo-soprano clef, 63
Middle C, 62, 79, 149, 153
Minor intervals (*see* Intervals, minor)
Minor triad (*see* Triads, minor)

Mixed groups (*see* Irregular groups)
Mixolydian mode, 554, 561, 564, 574, 609
Modes (*see* Church modes; *see also*
   specific entries, e. g., Dorian,
   Phrygian, etc.)
Musical terms, 336

Natural, 116, 120, 123, 125, 129
Natural harmonic series, 32-35
Natural minor scale (*see* Scales, natural
   minor)
Normal minor scale (*see* Scales, natural
   minor)
Notation of pitch (*see* Pitch, notation)
Note head, 252-259
Notes, 48-49, 251-277 (*see also* specific
   entries, e. g., Half note, Quarter
   note, etc.)
   division, 296-297, 316-317
   dotted, 288-290, 293-295
   names, 51-69
   relative duration, 331
   relative value, 269-277
   subdivision, 303-312

Octave, 11-16 (*see also* Intervals, octave)
Octave designations, 149-161
Octave duplications, 33
128th note, 251
128th rest, 278
One-line octave, 149-153, 161
Orchestration, 34
*Ottava* sign, 86-95
Overtones, 31-34 (*see also* Partials)

Parallel keys, 827-832, 834-835
Partials, 27-38
   distribution, 27, 36
   intensity, 27, 36, 38
Perfect intervals (*see* Intervals, perfect)
Phrygian mode, 554, 557, 565, 572
Pitch, 5-16, 25-26, 45
   notation, 46-161
Prime (*see* Intervals, unison)
Properties of sound, 39-40, 44-45
Pulse (*see* Beat)

Pure minor scale (*see* Scales, natural minor)
Pure sounds, 38

Quadruple meter (*see* Meter, quadruple)
Quality of sound (*see* Timbre)
Quarter note, 251-252
Quarter rest, 278, 280
Quintuple meter (*see* Meter, quintuple)

Rarefaction, 3
Relative keys, 789-806, 833-835
Rests, 278-294 (*see also* separate entries, e.g., Whole rest, Half rest, etc.)
  dotted, 288
  relative value, 284
Rhythm, 41-43
Root, 851, 860

Scale degrees, 549-552
Scales:
  basic, 541-580, 605
    modal names, 554
  chromatic, 144-148, 540
  definition, 144
  diatonic, 539-540, 710
  harmonic minor, 643-672, 817-821
  major, 583-623
  melodic minor, 673-705, 822-826
  natural minor, 626-642, 680-681, 816
  numbering of degrees, 548-549
Second (*see* Intervals, second)
Seventh (*see* Intervals, seventh)
Sharp, 116, 121
  use in chromatic scale, 144
Simple intervals (*see* Intervals, simple)
Simple time, 192-193, 196-197, 199, 201, 203-206, 230, 237, 239, 243, 245, 247, 249, 316, 337, 339, 370
Sixteenth note, 251, 257-258
Sixteenth rest, 278, 282
Sixth (*see* Intervals, sixth)
Sixty-fourth note, 251
Sixty-fourth rest, 278
Small octave, 154-157, 161
Softness (*see* Intensity)

Soprano clef, 63
Sound, 1-6, 8-10, 17-18, 20-25, 27, 31, 35-45
  generation, 1
  perception, 3-4
  sensation, 3
  transmission, 2-3, 17
Sound source, 1, 5, 19
Sound wave, 2-4, 12, 17, 19-20, 26
Spaces, 46-47, 50-51
  numbering, 50
Staff, 46-50, 71-73, 98-100
Standard of pitch, 13
Stem, 252-259
  length, 253
  placement, 253-255, 266-268
Stepwise, 536-539, 710-711
Stepwise succession of notes, 100, 108
Stress patterns (*see* Meter)
Stressed beats, 162-190
Strong beats, 166-190
Subcontra octave, 158-159, 161
Subdivision of beats (*see* Beat, subdivision)
Subdivision patterns, 405-413
Syncopation, 414-421

Tenor clef, 63-64, 67-69
Tension (*see* Stressed beats)
Terms (*see* Musical terms)
Tertian system, 839
Tetrachords, 616-623
  harmonic minor scale, 661
  major scale, 616-623
  melodic minor scale, 688-690
  natural minor scale, 632-634
Third (*see* Intervals, third)
Thirty-second note, 251
Thirty-second rest, 278, 283
*Three Blind Mice*, 202
Three-line octave, 149-151, 157, 161
Tie, 126, 128, 394-421
Timbre, 25-39, 45
Time, 40-43, 45
Time classification, 197-229, 366, 370, 373-374
  duple-compound, 198, 202, 206, 214
  duple-simple, 197, 205, 215

Time classification (continued)
  interpretation, 205-229
  quadruple-compound, 210
  quadruple-simple, 212
  quintuple-compound, 216
  quintuple-simple, 213
  triple-compound, 211
  triple-simple, 209
Time signatures, 339-394, 422-426
  compound time, 339, 346, 355, 357-361,
      374, 378
  simple time, 339, 345, 354, 373
Tonality, 713-714
Tone, 12-16 (*see also* Sound)
Tones, 48-49
Tonic-note (*see* Keynote)
Treble clef, 52-54, 60, 78
Triads, 838-954
  augmented, 849, 921-941
  basic, 840-848, 859, 873, 880, 896, 928
  definition, 838-839
  diminished, 849, 897-918

Triads (continued)
  major, 849-873
  minor, 849, 874-896
Triple meter (*see* Meter, triple)
Triplet, 230-231, 249 (*see also* Borrowed
      division)
Two-line octave, 149-152, 161

Unit, 313-331, 337-338, 353-365, 415
Upper tetrachord (*see* Tetrachords)

Vibrating body, 1, 4, 7-8
Vibration, 2, 12-14
Vibrational disturbance, 2-3, 20
Vibrations per second (*see* Frequency)

Weak beats, 166-190
Whole note, 251
Whole rest, 278
Whole-step, 96-100, 133, 547-548

*Yankee Doodle*, 201